The Origins
of Social Liberalism
in Germany

The Origins
of Social Liberalism
in Germany

DONALD G. ROHR

THE UNIVERSITY OF CHICAGO PRESS

CHICAGO AND LONDON

Library of Congress Catalog Card Number: 63-20914

THE UNIVERSITY OF CHICAGO PRESS, CHICAGO & LONDON
The University of Toronto Press, Toronto 5, Canada

To My Mother
and Father

Acknowledgments

My debts of gratitude to those who helped me prepare this monograph are many. I am particularly grateful to William L. Langer for suggesting a challenging subject. He has a rare ability to help students by stimulating and guiding rather than dominating their work. I also wish to thank James Phinney Baxter III, who as president of Williams College granted me leave to complete the research. Klaus Epstein, before and during our association in the Department of History at Brown University, was a constant source of advice and encouragement. I hope that they will accept this expression of thanks as more than a ritual offering.

D. G. R.

Providence, R. I.

Contents

Contents

Introduction

One of the great ironies of nineteenth-century European history was that the liberals, first in England, later in France and Germany, had to press their case for human progress through individual liberty at a time when economic progress and social welfare demanded more rather than fewer collective controls. The high degree of social organization required for industrial development, the growth of cities, the need for mass production and mass distribution to satisfy a mass market, meant that as men became increasingly dependent on each other, and as their collective activities and collective purposes increased, some measure of collectivist government was inevitable. But the liberals, as champions of individual rights and opponents of government authority, were understandably reluctant to modify their theories of political economy which emphasized the creative role of individual enterprise and denounced efforts at regulation by either the state or other corporate agencies. Gradually, however, modifications were made. The liberal movement detached itself from laissez faire theory and practice and evolved a "social liberalism" which in the first half of the twentieth century became a fixture in western Europe.[1] My purpose in this study is to examine the origins

[1] A good introduction to the historical problem is Harry K. Girvetz, *From Wealth to Welfare: The Evolution of Liberalism* (Stanford, Calif., 1950). Guido de Ruggiero, *The History of European Liberalism*, trans. R. G. Collingwood (Oxford, 1927), touches on the subject in several chapters, including one entitled "Social Liberalism," but does not deal with it in historical sequence.

1

of social liberalism as a school of thought in early nine-teenth-century Germany.

All too frequently, German liberals have been charac-terized as men obsessed with political and economic power and indifferent to social problems. This characterization needs to be corrected. As a stereotype it may apply to the party leaders of the late nineteenth century, but it should not be allowed to obscure the lively interest in social prob-lems displayed by liberal theorists of that time.[2] Nor should history be read backward so that the short-sighted leader-ship of the 1860's and later decades is taken as evidence of blindness earlier in the century. As early as the 1830's and 1840's, when Germany began to experience economic growth and social dislocation, men who were prominent in the liberal movement began to advocate such remedies as the graduated income tax, old-age pensions, insurance schemes for the sick and disabled, and wages and hours legislation — standard provisions of what has come to be known as the welfare state. Advocating these intervention-ist measures in response to the needs of the time, they de-clared their readiness to break with the doctrine of economic individualism, which had been twin brother to the liberal doctrine of limited, constitutional government.

The genealogy of these economic and constitutional doc-trines is easy to trace. They sprang from a common ethical ideal.

The idea of individual freedom constituted the essence of liberalism. It derived from the notion that the individual was the original and primary element, that the state and society therefore were based on individual wills. Liberalism would con-fer on every man the right . . . to develop according to his own coefficient of expansion.[3]

The German liberals found their ideal of individual liberty eloquently stated in the works of Immanuel Kant and Wil-

[2] Ruggiero, *European Liberalism*, pp. 265–70.

[3] Franz Schnabel, *Deutsche Geschichte im neunzehnten Jahrhundert* (Freiburg im Breisgau, 1929–36), II, 109–10.

helm von Humboldt.[4] They found the most systematic and persuasive exposition of economic individualism in Adam Smith's *The Wealth of Nations*. Indeed, Kantian philosophy did much to clear the way for the acceptance of Adam Smith's political economy.

The classical arguments of Smith's book — that the profit-maximizing individual was actually working for the good of society as a whole, that the state should not try to regulate artificially what "Nature" had ordained — presupposed many of the ethical principles which Smith had already outlined in his *Theory of Moral Sentiments*. There was also a very close correspondence between his principles and those of Immanuel Kant. Both Smith and Kant held that the goal of life was the self-realization of the individual through self-mastery. Both believed that the surest and most universal guides to right conduct were reason and conscience. Both held, accordingly, that it was every man's birthright, and his duty, to regulate his own life. Men who submitted meekly to external controls of any kind demeaned human nature. They should, of course, conduct themselves according to certain fundamental principles — i.e., Smith's "general rules," Kant's "categorical imperative." Otherwise society would dissolve into a chaos of conflicting wills. But a society where men acted on their natural impulses subject to the natural restraints of reason and conscience would be a society regulated by nature's laws rather than by the whim of a despot or the self-seeking of some interest group. An obvious sequence of ideas led from this ethical individualism to arguments for political and economic freedom.[5]

[4] On Kant and Humboldt, see Schnabel, *Deutsche Geschichte*, I, 290–93; Reinhold Aris, *History of Political Thought in Germany from 1789 to 1815* (London, 1936), pp. 65–105, 136–65; A. E. Teale, *Kantian Ethics* (Oxford, 1951), pp. 148–256. On the limitations of Kant's and Humboldt's individualism, see Leonard Krieger, *The German Idea of Freedom* (Boston, 1957), pp. 88–124, 166–73.

[5] Both the parallels and the differences between Adam Smith and Immanuel Kant are discussed in August Oncken, *Adam Smith und Immanuel*

The story of how Adam Smith's ideas were diffused in Germany, how they were simplified and distorted in the process, and how they inspired social and economic reforms has fascinated historians for some time.[6] Although *The Wealth of Nations* was translated into German immediately after publication in 1776, it attracted little notice until 1794, when a new and much improved translation appeared. About the same time three of the leading universities of northern Germany became centers for the propagation of Smith's ideas. The most notable of these was Goettingen where Georg Sartorius, a professor of history, inaugurated a course which was little more than an explication of Smith's theories. In 1796 Sartorius published a summary of those theories in the form of a students' manual. Meanwhile, at Koenigsberg, Christian Jakob Kraus, a professor of philosophy, made Smith's works the basis of a course which he taught from the mid-1790's until his death in 1807. And at Halle, from 1791 to 1827, Ludwig Heinrich Jakob taught a course which combined Kantian moral philosophy with a highly generalized resume of Smith's economic doctrine. Sartorius, Kraus, and Jakob prepared a generation of students for government ministries who, during the emergency created by Napoleon's invasions, found opportunities to put the ideas they had learned into practice.

Adam Smith's political economy found favor with these reformers on grounds other than its conformity with ante-

---

Kant (Leipzig, 1877), and in Judith Gruenfeld, *Die leitenden sozial- und wirtschaftspolitischen Ideen in der deutschen Nationaloekonomie und der Ueberwindung des Smithianismus* (Vienna, 1913), pp. 12–32.

[6] See Wilhelm Roscher, *Geschichte der National-Oekonomik in Deutschland* (Munich, 1874), 593–625, 651–700; Melchior Palyi, "The Introduction of Adam Smith on the Continent," in J. M. Clark *et al.*, *Adam Smith, 1776–1926* (Chicago, 1929), 180–233; Carl William Hasek, *The Introduction of Adam Smith's Doctrines into Germany* (New York, 1925); Wilhelm Treue, "Adam Smith in Deutschland," in Werner Conze (ed.), *Deutschland und Europa (Festschrift fuer Hans Rothfels)* (Dusseldorf, 1951), pp. 101–34.

cedent principles of ethical idealism. "Looked at from the present day, *The Wealth of Nations* . . . is a dynamic analysis and program of policy for an underdeveloped country."[7] At a time when England was heading anti-Napoleonic coalitions and acting as the paymaster of Europe, the English example seemed to prove that in freedom there was both strength and prosperity. The German reformers were convinced that the quickest way to promote economic growth and national power was to give free scope to individual profit-seeking by abolishing manorial and guild controls, encouraging local specialization, expanding markets, and dismantling trade barriers. Their assault on economic controls and hereditary social status combined with other impulses toward change, notably those of the "enlightened despots" of the later eighteenth century, to produce an "era of reform." The era of reform often identified with the work of Baron vom Stein and Prince Hardenberg in Prussia was actually much broader in scope. Every major state in Germany had its reformers in the opening decades of the nineteenth century.

By the 1830's the achievements of these liberal reformers, although still incomplete, had been put to the test of experience. In their first enthusiasm the reformers had predicted that the abolition of controls and the loosening of the social structure would allow both agriculture and the manufacturing trades to shift more readily into new methods of production, methods such as those which the English were developing so successfully. But by the 1830's social conditions in both England and Germany raised the question of whether these technological innovations, particularly the use of labor-saving machines in manufacture, were in fact desirable. By 1830 it was also clear that many Ger-

[7] W. W. Rostow, *The Process of Economic Growth* (New York, 1952), p. 6. German views on England are interestingly summarized in H. Pischke, *Die englische Industrierevolution im Spiegel der deutschen Reisebeschreibungen* (*1780–1825*) (Breslau, 1935).

man peasants had suffered rather than benefited from emancipation and land reform. Again, the weakening of the guilds seemed only to have depressed the artisan class. Meanwhile severe local hardships had resulted from the movement toward free trade within the new German Customs Union. It seemed as if the reformers had been misled by false hopes.

The German liberals had not only to answer these questions of fact, but also to meet a wide range of attacks aimed at the foundations of their liberal theory. Following the argument of J. G. Fichte that the individual is not self-sufficient, romantic-conservative philosophers, such as Adam Mueller, rejected the premises of liberal individualism. These philosophers denied that the individual was the primary element in society, argued that the self-fulfillment of the individual was possible only within the group, and concluded that the regulation of group life was the indispensable function of the all-encompassing group, the state.[8] Adam Smith and his German disciples were criticized by cameralists in Germany who pointed out the fallacy of erecting universal maxims of political economy on the limited experience of the British. In Britain itself, Thomas Malthus and David Ricardo undermined the liberals' confidence that nature's laws, operating freely, would ensure a desirable order in society. Their pessimistic

[8] Johann Gottlieb Fichte, *Saemmtliche Werke* (Berlin, 1845–46), III, 212–13; VI, 306. The passages referred to here occur in Fichte's *Grundlage des Naturrechts* (1796), and a lecture, "Ueber die Bestimmung des Menschens in der Gesellschaft" (1784). See also *Der geschlossene Handelsstaat* (1800), in *Werke*, III, 399–411; Adam Mueller, *Die Elemente der Staatskunst* (Berlin, 1809), I, 3–69. Malthus' influence in Germany is treated below in the section on population growth. See also Simon Nelson Patten, *Malthus and Ricardo* (Baltimore, 1889); Erich Theis, *David Ricardos Verkennung und Adam Muellers Erkenntnis der Wahrenkrisengruende ihrer Zeit* (Dueren, 1938) restates the corporatist views of the National Socialist period. On the penetration of French socialist ideas into Germany, see E. M. Butler, *The Saint-Simonian Religion in Germany* (Cambridge, 1926), pp. 52–59.

views, which quickly reached German readers, predicted a world in which nature's laws would keep the human race on the verge of starvation, would depress wages as population increased, and would guarantee an ever larger share in the national wealth to those who were already wealthy. Although the German reading public got its first systematic introduction to French socialist theories in Lorenz von Stein's *Der Socialismus und Communismus des heutigen Frankreiches* (1842), many socialist attacks on the irresponsibility of the liberals found echoes in German periodicals long before the appearance of Stein's book.

These questions and challenges, on the level of fact as well as on the level of theory, forced the German liberals to review their individualist premises and their objections to governmental regulation of social and economic affairs. Europeans generally had to come to terms with the facts of rapid and far-reaching social change during the post-Restoration period. They had to evaluate changes already made as a consequence of the French Revolution and the Napoleonic wars. They had to read portents of the change which would come about as the industrial revolution spread from Britain to the continent. In Germany, where the initial shock of revolutionary change was less drastic and its progress less advanced than in France or Britain, a large number of observers were able to study the evidence of change around them with an unusual mixture of concern and scholarly detachment. Liberals and conservatives alike in Germany felt that with England and France as models the forces of change could be mastered and directed to their country's advantage. Many liberals welcomed, even fostered, industrial development, confident that with proper precautions Germany could enjoy the benefits of industrialization without suffering the distress which by that time was so manifest in England. If these precautions required government action, curtailment of individual rights, or abridgment of free enterprise, then so much the worse for free enterprise. Their conviction that industrial development could be controlled and society safeguarded against the misery which had beset industrial workers in England was a striking anticipation of the present-day assumption that industrial development will cure rather than create social ills among poor and backward peoples.

The original works of German social liberalism which emerged from the effort to adjust liberal theories to the observable facts of the 1830's and 1840's have been strangely neglected by historians. A recent anthology of source material for the history of the social problem in Germany between 1800 and 1870 has ignored them altogether.[9] In a still more recent and more specialized collection of documents, the Marxist historian, Juergen Kuczynski, published a number of extracts from these works together with comments indicating that he considers them his discoveries. Occasionally writers on the period just before the outbreak of revolution in 1848 noted, with little accuracy, the emergence of social liberalism, and then dismissed it as unimportant. Friedrich Engels, in one of the reports on the revolution which he wrote as Karl Marx's ghost, observed that by 1847 "there was hardly a single prominent political character among the bourgeoisie who did not proclaim himself a 'Socialist' in order to insure himself the sympathy of the proletarian class."[10] Heinrich von Treitschke, in the final volume of his *History of Germany in the Nineteenth Century*, deals at some length with the reaction against Adam Smith's "unhistorical optimism," but of the liberals' second thoughts on social policy he says only: "Even

[9] Ernst Schraepler (ed.), *Quellen zur Geschichte der sozialen Frage in Deutschland* (Goettingen, 1955); Juergen Kuczynski, *Die Geschichte der Lage der Arbeiter unter dem Kapitalismus*, Vol. IX: *Buergerliche und halbfeudale Literatur aus den Jahren 1840 bis 1847 zur Lage der Arbeiter* (Berlin, 1960).

[10] Karl Marx (Friedrich Engels), *Revolution and Counter-Revolution in Germany in 1848* (New York, 1896), p. 23.

among the wealthy Rhenish middle class, widely and pop-
ularly known as the 'Cologne clique,' there was a lingering,
feeble, and purely theoretical fondness for social radical-
ism."[11]

In the conclusion of this study I have suggested some
reasons why the pioneers of social liberalism in Germany
attracted so little attention. I shall now discuss the views
of an American historian who has misunderstood rather
than ignored them. Theodore S. Hamerow, in his *Restoration, Revolution, Reaction,* has combined comprehensive
scholarship with an imaginative prose style and has offered
some very sharp insights into the social forces underlying
political development in Germany between 1815 and 1871.
Unfortunately, he has drawn too simple an equation between the liberal movement and middle-class interests and
has defined those interests too narrowly as "cautious constitutionalism and unrestricted industrialism."[12] No matter
how unanimously the liberals may have agreed on the necessity for gradual constitutional change, they certainly
did not agree with each other on economic and social policies. Ludolf Camphausen, one of the prominent liberals
cited by Professor Hamerow, far from favoring "unrestricted industrialism," spoke out against industrial development in the course of the 1840's. Others, including
Gustav Mevissen and Karl Biedermann, openly acknowledged the need for controlling industrialism in the public
interest. Both Mevissen and Biedermann were profoundly
influenced in their thinking by socialist denunciations of the
evils of unrestricted individualism. Many radical democrats in southern Germany, men such as Gustav von Struve,
were similarly influenced. Professor Hamerow's statement

[11] Heinrich von Treitschke, *Deutsche Geschichte im neunzehnten Jahrhundert* (Leipzig, 1927), V, 508.
[12] Theodore S. Hamerow, *Restoration, Revolution, Reaction: Economics
and Politics in Germany, 1815–1871* (Princeton, N.J., 1958). The passages
referred to here occur chiefly in the chapter on "The Ideological Conflict,"
pp. 56–74.

that they ". . . were separated from the socialists by an impassable ideological gulf . . ." is misguided.[13]

Much of this misunderstanding of liberal views on social problems results from Professor Hamerow's interpretation of the problems themselves. Having dwelled on the hardships caused by liberal agrarian reforms, having described the advent of industrialism as exclusively serving the interest of the middle class and bringing *only* ruin to the artisans, having underemphasized the role of population growth as a cause of social distress, and having ignored evidence of rising living standards in the country as a whole, Professor Hamerow describes the liberals as holding that "poverty and hunger were part of the game; they were the price which society must pay for industrial progress."[14] Poverty and hunger *were* a part of the German scene in the 1830's and 1840's. But these conditions were not as unrelieved as Professor Hamerow suggests. Nor did the liberals accept social distress as an inevitable consequence of their economic policies. Quite the contrary, their policies were aimed at increasing production of food and manufactures. What better way is there to relieve the pressures of rapid population growth? One of the great issues in the 1830's and 1840's was whether the interests of society as a whole would be better served by further encouragement to free enterprise or by curbing its excesses. It would be naïve and unhistorical to imply that all the liberals were concerned solely for the general welfare. But it would be equally naïve and unhistorical to characterize them as so avid for profit, so selfish and exploitative, that the hunger

[13] *Ibid.*, p. 67. The same sort of error recurs later where the author alludes to Disraeli's "writing about the two nations, the rich and the poor, separated from each other by an impassable gulf of resentment." The whole point of Disraeli's *Sybil, or the Two Nations* was that the gulf between rich and poor was *not* impassable. The marriage of Egremont and Sybil symbolizes the union of the classes; the career of Devilsdust shows how class lines could be crossed.

[14] *Ibid.*, p. 63.

and poverty of their fellow Germans were shrugged off as "part of the game."

Clearly, no appraisal of liberal ideas on social problems is possible without a balanced understanding of the problems themselves. I have therefore begun my discussion of these ideas with a first chapter which outlines the uneven course of economic development in early nineteenth-century Germany followed by a second chapter which sketches the great diversity of social conditions in the 1830's and 1840's. The German liberals whose ideas are treated in subsequent chapters were selected for their prominence; but I have not tried to measure the extent of their influence. My object has been, rather, to show how they adjusted their thinking on social problems to the social realities of their time. These liberals are difficult to classify into schools of thought; indeed, they show an appropriately high degree of individuality in their thinking. I have distinguished two groups: those who emphasized the beneficial effects of free enterprise and argued for extending or maintaining it; and those who accepted the necessity of government regulation in the interests of social welfare and were primarily concerned with the scope of such regulation. Between chapters devoted to these two viewpoints, I have inserted a third which examines the divergent views of German liberals as they appeared in a common meeting place, the *Staatslexikon* of Karl von Rotteck and Karl Welcker. Frontiers of time and place are always somewhat arbitrary in intellectual history. I have limited this discussion to the German states which were later incorporated into the Hohenzollern empire. I have set 1847 as a terminal date because the tumultuous events of the following years created a very different intellectual atmosphere.

I

Economic Changes

In 1846 Wilhelm Dieterici, who was then head of the Prussian Bureau of Statistics, published a study in which he compared figures of production and consumption for 1805 to 1806 with those figures for the 1830's and 1840's. He concluded that the economic changes of the forty years from 1805 to 1845, particularly the growth in productivity, had effected a "complete revolution" (*Umschwung*). Dieterici exaggerated; in view of the more rapid changes which came after 1850, the word "revolution" is hardly applicable to his period. The years which he describes were instead a time when traditional ways were being abandoned while new directions had not yet emerged. W. W. Rostow calls this stage of economic growth one of the "pre-conditions for take-off: the transitional era when a society prepares itself — or is prepared by external forces — for sustained growth."[1]

Around the turn of the century, a series of liberal reforms began to make drastic changes in the forms of landholding and in the organization of the manufacturing and service trades. These reforms in turn encouraged the introduction of new methods in agriculture and of mechanical inventions in industry, innovations which began to transform habits of work which had remained unchanged for genera-

[1] W. W. Rostow, *The Stages of Economic Growth* (Cambridge, Eng., 1960), p. 17. Wilhelm Dieterici, *Der Volkswohlstand im preussischen Staate* (Berlin, 1846) is a progress report by a pioneer in the field of social statistics. Remarks on its value will be found in chap. ii.

tions. Then, with the formation of the German Customs Union (*Zollverein*) and the mechanization of transport, physical and legal barriers to free exchange within Germany began to fall, and the prospect of a mass market took shape for the first time in the country's history. Finally, all the German states at this time were experiencing sudden rises in population, rises which both resulted from and forced the pace of other economic change.

POPULATION GROWTH

In the course of the nineteenth century almost all European countries underwent rapid population growth, and Germany was no exception.[2] In 1815 the German states which later made up the Second Empire, excluding Alsace-Lorraine, had a total population of some 22,700,000. During the next three decades the population grew by 38.5 per cent, an increase which resulted almost exclusively from an excess of births over deaths. There was some immigration, but it was so small as to be negligible. The rate of population growth shot up immediately after the Napoleonic wars, dipped sharply in the 1830's and rose again in the 1840's. The rise and fall of the Prussian rate of increase during the first half of the century was typical. The average annual excess of births over deaths for 1,000 of population in Prussia was 15.2 between 1816 and 1820 and 16.6 between 1821 and 1825. This rate was cut in half during the 1830's but rose again to 13.5 in the years 1841 and 1845. The rate of increase in Saxony at this time was somewhat higher than in Prussia; in Bavaria and Wuerttemberg

[2] Most demographers agree that this growth was the climax of a movement which began before 1750, primarily because of a drop in the death rate which in turn resulted from technological progress and higher living standards. It is also possible that the fertility rate rose at this time because easier material circumstances permitted earlier marriage. See R. R. Kuczynski, *Population Movements* (Oxford, 1936), pp. 23–25; A. M. Carr-Saunders, *World Population* (Oxford, 1936), pp. 60–63; Marcel Reinhard, *Histoire de la population mondiale de 1700 à 1948* (Paris, 1949), p. 168.

it was somewhat lower. But all of the states followed the same general curve.

The importance of these figures for this study is that they reveal that the high rate of increase in the decade after 1815 created a "population bulge," or "birth cohort," which began to reach maturity by the late 1830's. The fact that this generation reached child-bearing age by that time helps to explain the higher rate of population increase between 1841 and 1845, which reversed the downward trend of the preceding decade. And, since a German boy was usually considered ready for full-time employment after his fifteenth birthday, there was, in the 1830's an extraordinarily heavy demand for jobs; there was the threat of crowding on the land and in the trades and the immediate prospect of what is now called "disguised unemployment."

The rate of population growth varied not only from decade to decade but from place to place. Between 1830 and 1849 the population of Prussia grew by 25 per cent and that of Saxony by 30 per cent, while that of Wuerttemberg grew by 11 per cent and that of Bavaria by only 6.6 per cent.[3] The north-south pattern which appears in these figures is no more striking than the difference between east and west which appears in another set of figures. The twenty administrative districts of Prussia which lay within the Germanic Confederation had an average annual increase of 1.37 per cent during the years from 1834 to 1852. But the eastern and central districts recorded annual increases which were well above the average, while those in the west fell considerably below it. For example, the eastern districts of Koeslin and Stettin had an average annual increase of 2.03 per cent and 1.83 per cent, respectively, while the district of Trier had an average annual increase of 0.86 per cent, and the district of Muenster, 0.41 per cent.

[3] Paul Mombert, *Bevoelkerungslehre* (Jena, 1929), pp. 182–83; August Loesch, *Bevoelkerungswellen und Wechsellagen* (Jena, 1936), pp. 12–15. See also Mombert's earlier collection, *Studien zur Bevoelkerungsbewegung in Deutschland* (Karlsruhe, 1907).

The population of Germany north of the Main and east of the Weser was growing more rapidly at this time than the population of the south and west because the latter areas were already densely populated. The only break in this pattern was the kingdom of Saxony which, as we shall see, had not only the fastest rate of growth but also the heaviest density. Table 1 shows the different population densities of the five major states in the period 1815 to 1850.[4]

TABLE 1

POPULATION DENSITY

(Number of Inhabitants per Square Kilometer)

State	1815	1830	1850
Prussia	35	44	56
Saxony	78	93	126
Bavaria	48	54	59
Wuerttemberg	72	81	89
Baden	66	79	90

Since the German economy in the early nineteenth century remained predominantly agricultural, the population increases which came at that time had to be absorbed on the farms and in the villages and small towns. Urbanization had hardly begun in Germany before 1850. To be sure, the number of townspeople grew somewhat more rapidly in the 1830's and 1840's than did the number of country dwellers. Saxony, with the heaviest urban concentration of any German state counted 27 per cent of the population as city dwellers in 1834 and some 33.3 per cent in 1849. But in Bavaria, where the cities were growing at a rate triple that of the rural districts, the city population in 1852 was still only 11.2 per cent of the whole. In Prussia the balance between town and country populations showed very little change in these decades. In 1834, 25.6 per cent of the population could be classified as urban, in 1849, 26.7 per cent.[5]

[4] Figures on local differences are from Friedrich von Reden, *Erwerbs- und Verkehrsstatistik von Koenigstaats Preussen* (Darmstadt, 1853–54), I, 27.

[5] Adna F. Weber, *The Growth of Cities in the Nineteenth Century* (New York, 1899), pp. 82–94; Ernst Engel, "Das Anwachsen der Bevoel-

Furthermore the "urban" population of pre-industrial Germany lived in small towns. The figures given here for urban dwellers in Prussia and Saxony take into account all those who were living in cities with a population of 2,000 or more. Bavarian officials defined their cities not by the number of inhabitants but by legal status. Of the fifty-two Bavarian cities so defined, thirty had populations of 5,000 or less. Medium-sized cities (20,000 to 100,000 inhabitants) and large cities (100,000 inhabitants or more) taken together accounted for only 3.7 per cent of the population of Bavaria in 1852, 4.7 per cent of the Prussian population in 1849, and 9.9 per cent of the population of Saxony in 1849. These figures should be contrasted with those for England and Wales, where in 1851 34 per cent of the population lived in cities with populations greater than 20,000.[6] The effect of population growth in Germany, then, was not so much to spawn city proletariats, or to duplicate the urban squalor of industrial Britain, as it was to crowd the countryside.

The rise of an overseas emigration movement was unmistakable evidence of population pressures in Germany before 1850. Between 1820 and 1829 fewer than 10,000 emigrants left Germany to settle abroad. In the 1830's their number rose to 143,060, and in the 1840's to 425,200. No doubt religious or political motives prompted some of these emigrants to leave their *Heimat*, but the great majority of them went in search of better economic opportunities in countries where land was plentiful and cheap and where labor was scarce and well paid. As might be

---

kerung im preussischen Staate seit 1816," *Zeitschrift des koeniglich preussischen Statistischen Bureaus*, I, (1861), p. 29. T. S. Hamerow, citing conditions in Saxony and the rise of Berlin, rather overstates the case when he says that in the 1840's "the difference in size between the rural and urban population was rapidly diminishing." See his *Restoration, Revolution, Reaction: Economics and Politics in Germany, 1815–1871* (Princeton, N.J., 1958), p. 20.

[6] Great Britain, *Census of Great Britain in 1851* (London, 1854), p. 14.

expected, most of the emigrants left from those states in southwestern Germany which had the thickest population densities. Between 1841 and 1850 the average annual excess of emigrants over immigrants for 1,000 of population was 0.8 in Prussia, 2.6 in Bavaria, 3.9 in Wuerttemberg, 5.0 in Baden, and 5.7 in the grand duchy of Hesse.[7]

Further evidence of the economic strain caused by population growth appears in German legislation. After the Thirty Years' War had depopulated central Europe, German cameralists of the seventeenth and eighteenth centuries and the princes whom they advised tried to restore the populations of their states by forbidding emigration and by encouraging early marriage. But early in the nineteenth century these policies were either suspended or reversed. Beginning with Baden in 1808, the legal barriers to emigration were gradually lowered in one state after another. And by the 1830's the overcrowded duchies and kingdoms of the south and west began to help emigrants on their way by putting them into contact with reliable shippers, or, as was the case in Baden, by helping them to raise passage money. Meanwhile a large number of states enacted laws to restrict marriage. After 1825 the government of Bavaria required applicants for marriage to pass a means test. During the 1830's Baden, Wuerttemberg, and half a dozen smaller states followed suit. These laws did succeed in somewhat reducing the number of marriages. The marriage rates in Bavaria, Baden, and Wuerttemberg were 15 per cent lower than those in Prussia and Saxony where restrictions were not in force. But these restrictive laws were at best only partly successful in checking population growth. The rate of illegitimate

[7] Wilhelm Moenckmeier, *Die deutsche ueberseeische Auswanderung* (Jena, 1912), pp. 14–29; Georg von Mayr, *Statistik und Gesellschaftslehre* (2d ed.; Tuebingen, 1914–26), II, 635. For an introduction to "emigration literature," see Paul C. Weber, *America in Imaginative German Literature in the First Half of the Nineteenth Century* (New York, 1926), pp. 201–34.

births in Bavaria during the 1840's was triple that in Prussia.[8]

One historian has attributed these clumsy efforts to control population increases to the influence of Malthusian theory on German bureaucrats.[9] A translation of the *Essay on Population* had been available to German readers since 1807, and Malthus' views were widely discussed. In the next few decades a torrent of books, pamphlets, and articles on the population problem came off the German press. One of these volumes, to cite an extreme case, was the work of a physician who solemnly proposed to revive the old Roman practice of infibulation and put seals on the sex organs of all males who were old enough to sire children but too poor to support them.

Malthus' *Essay* alone did not cause anxiety. Rather, his theory made so deep an impression because it seemed to explain observable facts of population growth and because it expressed fears already present in Germany. Long before Malthus, indeed as early as the 1780's, some German cameralists had warned against overpopulation. By the 1830's, that threat had become a reality in the south and west. It is unlikely that the thousands of peasants and artisans who left Baden, Wuerttemberg, and Hesse at that time did so

[8] On emigration policies, see Moenckmeier, *Auswanderung*, pp. 228–31; Eugen von Philippovich (ed.), "Auswanderung und Auswanderungspolitik," *Schriften des Vereins fuer Sozialpolitik*, LII (1892), 131–34, 189–204, 264; Marcus Lee Hansen, *The Atlantic Migration* (Cambridge, Mass., 1940), pp. 7–8. On laws restricting marriage, see Karl Braun, "Das Zwangszoelibat fuer Mittellose in Deutschland," *Vierteljahrschrift fuer Volkswirtschaft und Kulturgeschichte*, XX (1867), 1–80; Friedrich Thudichum, *Ueber unzulaessige Beschraenkungen des Rechts der Verehelichung* (Tuebingen, 1866), pp. 31–87, 121–35; Arthur Freiherr von Fircks, *Bevoelkerungslehre und Bevoelkerungspolitik* (Leipzig, 1898), pp. 159, 206.

[9] Ludwig Elster, "Bevoelkerungswesen," *Handwoerterbuch der Staatswissenschaften*, ed. Johannes Conrad and Ludwig Elster (3d ed.; Jena, 1909–11), II, 960. A useful bibliography of material on the population problem which appeared early in the century was published in *Deutsche Vierteljahrschrift*, III (1844), 98–141. The proposal for infibulation was made by Karl August Weinhold in his *Von der Uebervoelkerung in Mittel-Europa* (Halle, 1827).

because they had been reading Malthus. By the 1830's everywhere in Germany an unusually large "birth cohort" was coming of age and had created an unprecedented demand for jobs. The population increases which caused this pressure for land to farm and trades to ply coincided with the liberal reform measures which were breaking down the traditional social and economic cadres of guild and manor. In the long run, of course, the new mobility brought about by liberal reforms created opportunities for the solution of the population problem. But the immediate effect of the reforms was to destroy old forms of social and economic security at a time when rapid population growth was putting the country under severe economic strain.

LIBERAL REFORMS

The liberal reforms of the late eighteenth and early nineteenth centuries were the work of men who believed that in freedom there is strength. Expected to produce more loyal subjects and more dependable soldiers, the reforms, as they bore directly on the economy, aimed at releasing the energies of economic self-interest in a competitive system.[10] For those engaged in the trades and services, the reformers proposed *Gewerbefreiheit*, freedom for each individual to choose his own line of work, freedom to enter any trade he pleased. *Gewerbefreheit* entailed the dissolution of the guilds as regulatory bodies. This meant the abolition of local privileges, monopolies, and guild restrictions with respect to the numbers of artisans and tradesmen and the methods of production which they employed. Reforms were also proposed for the landed population. The reformers proposed to abolish manorial servitudes and communal obligations, to destroy the corporate form of

[10] Heinrich Bechtel, *Wirtschaftsgeschichte Deutschlands* (Munich, 1951–56), III, 195–219; Friedrich Luetge, *Deutsche Sozial- und Wirtschaftsgeschichte* (2d ed.; Berlin, 1960), pp. 379–81; Werner Conze, "Die Wirkungen der liberalen Agrarreformen auf die Volksordnung in Mitteleuropa im neunzehnten Jahrhundert," *Vierteljahrschrift fuer Sozial- und Wirtschaftsgeschichte*, XXXVIII (1949), 1–47.

German agriculture and convert the peasants into independent, self-reliant individuals. Unhindered and unsupported by manorial lords or neighbors, individual farmers would be careful in the planning of their harvests or in the breeding of their livestock; they would work hard in their own interest and would consequently produce more abundantly for the common good.

The goal of the agrarian reformers was to convert the peasants' land titles from dependent tenure to direct ownership and in this manner to emancipate the peasants from manorial labor services and dues, from the jurisdiction of patrimonial courts, and from legal restrictions on their rights to move, to marry, to choose a vocation, or to own property. This emancipation (*Bauernbefreiung*) was to be accompanied by another process called *Separation* which included the division of common property and common rights (*Gemeinheitsteilung*) and the consolidation of scattered landholdings into compact, individually owned units (*Zusammenlegung*). How well all of these reforms succeeded in establishing a new society of small, freeholding farmers is a question of extraordinary complexity. The customs, practices, and legal forms which had to be abolished were very old and very local in character. Reform measures were enacted at different times and were applied on different schedules to different classes of peasants in the various German states. Historians usually point out the great contrast between the course of agrarian reform east of the Elbe and that which took effect in southern and western Germany. But the reform laws and their results varied tremendously, not simply between one state and another, but also between localities and classes of peasants within individual jurisdictions.

By 1830, as the result of a process which had begun in some parts of the country in the late eighteenth century, most of western, central, and southern Germany had abolished serfdom as a legal status. The emancipation laws which had been enacted in these states prescribed financial settlements whereby a peasant could acquire full title to his land and be freed of traditional obligations by paying a compensatory fee to his *Grundherr*. Depending on the region, the redemption fee equalled anywhere from ten to twenty-four times the total value of the peasant's annual obligations.[11] There was constant pressure on the governments of the various states to revise the amounts and schedules of redemption payments, either upward or downward, so the work of emancipation proceeded at a very irregular pace. The redemption law of 1832 in Saxony was probably the most generous of any German state. The grand duchy of Hesse and the kingdom of Hanover completed their legislation in the 1830's and moved quite rapidly toward making it effective. But the process of emancipation, which had been off to an early start in southern Germany under enlightened princes of the previous century, was retarded by the princes and imperial knights who had been mediatized after 1803. Families such as the Hohenlohes and Sayn-Wittgensteins would not allow the governments in Munich, Stuttgart, or Karlsruhe, to come between them and their peasants. Even when they lost a legislative battle, as they did in Wuerttemberg in 1836, they continued to obstruct the execution of the laws until frightened off by local peasant risings in 1848.[12]

In Prussia the progress of emancipation was almost as diverse as the character of the lands which the Hohenzol-

[11] Friedrich Luetge, *Die Mitteldeutsche Grundherrschaft* (Jena, 1934); Adolph Thomas, *Beitraege zur Geschichte der Bauernbefreiung und der Entlastung des laendlichen Grundbesitzes im Grossherzogtum Hessen* (Mainz, 1910); Werner Wittich, *Die Grund-Herrschaft in Nordwest Deutschland* (Leipzig, 1896); Otto Reinhard, *Die Grundentlastung in Wuerttemberg* (Tuebingen, 1910); Sebastien Hausmann, *Die Grundentlastung in Bayern* (Strasburg, 1892); Otto Stoltz, "Die Bauernbefreiung in Sueddeutschland im Zusammenhang der Geschichte," *Deutsche Vierteljahrschrift fuer Sozial- und Wirtschaftsgeschichte*, XXXIII (1940), 1–68.

[12] Reinhard, *Grundentlastung in Wuerttemberg*, pp. 20–41; Hausmann, *Grundentlastung in Bayern*, pp. 131–40; Friedrich Lautenschlager, *Die Agrarunruhen in den badischen Standes- und Grundherrschaften im Jahre 1848* (Heidelberg, 1895), pp. 7–24.

lerns had annexed. Peasants in the western provinces, who after 1813 had been forced to give up the gains in legal and economic status made under French law during the Napoleonic occupation, took the outbreak of the July Revolution in France as a signal to demonstrate their grievances. In 1833 the government in Berlin finally placated these peasants with a redemption law which made emancipation in the Prussian Rhineland and Westphalia, as elsewhere in western Germany, a simple matter of financing. In the five eastern provinces, however, where for several hundred years peasants had been held firmly under manorial control, emancipation was far more complex.[13] The celebrated Edict of 1807, which abolished serfdom in all of Prussia (which was still under royal control), affected all of the peasants. But further legislation was needed to define the conditions under which they could improve their titles to land, and this legislation discriminated among the peasants according to their wealth and form of tenure.

The most favored class of peasants in the eastern provinces was made up of those who were sufficiently well off to own draft animals and who held their land by a fairly secure tenure even before 1807. These peasants, who numbered about 175,000 in 1820, were allowed by a law of 1821 to free themselves of residual dues and labor services by payment of a redemption fee, and before 1848, some 171,351 peasants in this class had elected to do so. A second class was made up of those peasants who owned their own teams of horses, or yokes of oxen, but who held their land by a precarious title. They were allowed to convert their tenure to direct ownership and to be free of labor services under two edicts, one issued in 1811, the other in 1816. These edicts outlined a process of emancipation,

[13] Theodor von der Goltz, *Geschichte der deutschen Landwirtschaft* (Stuttgart, 1902–03), II, 130–204; Georg Friedrich Knapp, *Die Bauernbefreiung und der Ursprung der Landarbeiter in den aelteren Teilen Preussens* (2d ed.; Munich, 1927).

known in this instance as *Regulierung*, or *Regulation*, whereby the peasant surrendered one-third of his land (if he had heritable title to it), or one-half of his land (if his title were non-heritable), to his *Gutsherr*. These edicts, it should be noted, applied to only about 100,00 proprietors. That the terms they laid down were onerous is indicated by the fact that as late as 1848 nearly 30,000 of these peasants had chosen to retain their old dependent tenure rather than give up so large a portion of their land.[14] The third and by far the largest class of peasants in Brandenburg, Silesia, Pomerania, and East Prussia were those who were too poor to have their own draft animals. This class, estimated at some 60 per cent of the total peasant population in the five eastern provinces, was not provided for in any of the edicts which followed the abolition of serfdom. Although they had lost the legal status of serfs, they continued to owe heavy labor services to their landlords and to live under their jurisdiction. Meanwhile in 1808 they had lost the security which had been afforded them by *Bauernschutz*, a ban on the revocation of leases and the acquisition of peasant land by the upper classes which had been issued by Frederick II in an effort to prevent land-hungry masters from squeezing the peasants out of their holdings.

"For whosoever hath, to him shall be given", if not the intention, was the eventual direction of Prussia's agrarian reforms. The poor tended to lose what little they had. Many of those who were eligible for *Regulation* were finally forced by the required sacrifice of land to sell out everything. Meanwhile the poorest class of peasants were forced out of their leaseholds, so that hundreds of thousands of acres of peasant land could be appropriated by

[14] Knapp, *Bauernbefreiung*, I, 256–69. Additional statistics are taken from Alexander von Lengerke, *Landwirtschaftliche Statistik der deutschen Bundesstaaten* (Brunswick, 1840–41), I, 481; August Meitzen, *Der Boden und die landwirtschaftlichen Verhaeltnisse des preussischen Staates* (Berlin, 1868–71), IV, 302.

large landowners. Whether the reforms created a rural proletariat in Prussia is debatable, but no one can seriously question the judgment that ". . . the consequences were disastrous from the point of view of creating a large, independent and reasonably prosperous peasant class. . . ."[15] Peasant emancipation no doubt encouraged a more efficient agriculture by enabling estate-owners and well-to-do peasants to increase their acreages, but this gain in efficiency was made at the expense of thousands of the poorer peasants who were "emancipated" into the status of landless wageworkers.

The process of breaking up communal farming was as patchy in execution as that of peasant emancipation. The division of commons (*Gemeinheitsteilung*) was usually the sharing of pasture, meadow, and woodlot among those who had traditional rights to use them. But in some regions it included the splitting up of *Allmenden*, or property owned by a corporation of shareholders. In southern Germany where *Allmenden* were numerous, and where the loss of rights of commons would have meant near-starvation to many peasants, legislation before 1848 served only to guarantee and define their rights. But in northern Germany division of commons was far advanced by the 1840's. In 1802 the kingdom of Hanover, where English influence was strong, provided a model ordinance for the process, a model which was followed by subsequent legislation in Prussia (1821), and Saxony (1832). This legislation provided some safeguards to those who had rights of com-

---

[15] Walter M. Simon, *The Failure of the Prussian Reform Movement, 1807–1819* (Ithaca, 1955), p. 100. The passage cited refers to the edicts of 1811 and 1816 but is apposite to the whole history of emancipation. For a mid-century review of the reforms, see Peter Reichensperger, *Die Agrarfrage* (Trier, 1847), pp. 294–339. G. F. Knapp argued that the reforms did produce a rural proletariat, in his *Bauernbefreiung*, I, 306–7. Other historians have pointed to the existence of landless day laborers in Prussia before the reforms and have accounted for the growth of this class in the nineteenth century by citing the general population increases. See Theodor von der Goltz, *Die laendliche Arbeiterklasse und der preussische Staat* (Jena, 1893), p. 85; Conze, "Wirkungen," pp. 21–23.

mons. Division was not compulsory unless half of those
with rights declared in favor of it. Nevertheless, where
large landholders were powerful, as they were east of the
Elbe, division was forced through rapidly, even ruthlessly.
In central and eastern Prussia less than a half-million peasants were eligible to improve their tenure before 1848, but
by that time nearly a million had had their rights altered
by division of commons.[16]

Liberal efforts to reform the trades and services, like liberal agrarian reforms, ran an uneven course. Except for
those parts of Germany where *Gewerbefreiheit* had been
imposed by French occupying authorities under the Le
Chapelier law of 1791, Prussia went furthest toward
breaking up the guilds in the first half of the century.[17]
In 1810 Prince Hardenberg set reform in motion with a
trade tax edict which, in addition to levying taxes on business enterprises according to their size, began to simplify
licensing procedures. A later trade tax law in 1820 dis-
pensed with licensing altogether except for peddlers. The
law of 1810 meanwhile had been supplemented by a police
law of 1811 which required anyone engaged in trade or
manufacture to have the status of townsman (*Burgher*)
but did away with requirements of guild membership. The
law further provided that guild members could resign, and
that guild members could work for non-guild members

[16] Goltz, *Geschichte*, II, 146–60; Ludwig Elster, "Gemeinheiten, Gemeinheitsteilung," *Handwoerterbuch der Staatswissenschaften*, ed. Ludwig Elster and Johannes Conrad (4th ed.; Jena, 1923–28), IV, 846–48;
Franz Christoph, *Die laendlichen Gemeingueter (Allmenden) in Preussen*
(Jena, 1906); Franz X. Wismueller, *Geschichte der Teilung der Gemein-
laendereien in Bayern* (Stuttgart, 1904). The estimate of the numbers
affected in Prussia is from Meitzen, *Boden*, IV, 302–3. Very little progress
was made toward consolidation of scattered landholdings into compact
units until much later in the century. See Bruno Schlitte, *Die Zusammenlegung der Grundstuecke* (Leipzig, 1886); Adolf Muenzinger, *Die Flurbe-
reinigung in Sueddeutschland* (Berlin, 1936), pp. 12–17.

[17] Kurt von Rohrscheidt, *Vom Zunftzwang zur Gewerbefreiheit* (Berlin,
1898), pp. 476–512; Hugo C. M. Wendel, *The Evolution of Industrial
Freedom in Prussia, 1845–1849* (New York, 1921), pp. 1–16.

without losing their guild rights. The law set up procedures whereby the guilds could dissolve themselves, or could be dissolved by police ordinance. And, finally, it abolished wage and price regulations.

The laws of 1810 and 1811 applied, of course, only to those provinces which were actually controlled by the Prussian government at that time. After 1813, *Gewerbefreiheit*, in its French form, remained in force in the Rhineland and Westphalia. Brandenburg, Pomerania, Silesia, and East Prussia observed the reforms of 1810–11, while Posen and the newly acquired province of Saxony continued to enforce guild regulations. In 1820, Hardenberg promised to make the laws uniform for the entire kingdom, but he died with his promise unfulfilled. This heterogeneity in Prussian commercial law lasted until 1845 when an *Allgemeine Gewerbeordung*, or universal trade law, was introduced.[18] The new law was a victory, although not a total one, for the advocates of *Gewerbefreiheit*. Provincial and municipal financial officers, as well as guilds, lost their rights to grant concessions to, and collect fees from, those who wished to engage in trade. Monopolies were abolished except for the holders of patent rights. Price regulations were abolished except where they applied to the sale of food in shops or restaurants. Licenses were to be required only of itinerants, such as peddlers and repairmen. The status of townsman was no longer a prerequisite for becoming a license-holder. The non-itinerant trades (*stehende Gewerbe*), therefore, were open to anyone who could secure a police certificate. The old guilds were directed to bring their constitutions and bylaws into conformity with the new law which also provided for the founding of new guilds with primarily educational or charitable functions. Relations between employers and employees were to be regulated by contract, or by guild rules,

[18] Wendel, *Industrial Freedom*, pp. 17–41; Hugo Roehl, *Beitraege zur preussischen Handwerkerpolitik vom Allgemeinen Landrecht bis zur Allgemeinen Gewerbeordnung von 1845* (Leipzig, 1900), pp. 189–271.

or, where neither of these applied, by government directives.

The experience of Bavaria with *Gewerbefreiheit* illustrates very well the difficulties of making this break with the past.[19] Only in the Bavarian Pfalz, where French reforms remained the law after 1813, was the power of the guilds broken. In Bavaria proper, the ministry of Count Max Montgelas between 1799 and 1812 deprived the guilds of their regulatory powers and vested those powers in the government. In 1806, Montgelas announced that he favored the abolition of all regulation, but he failed to enact any such measure before 1817 when he was forced out of office. Widespread dissatisfaction with state supervision of trade and manufacture led in 1825 to some relaxation of state control, but this brought numerous complaints from the guilds, in particular the complaint that free entry into trades was resulting in the flooding of the trades with more tradesmen than the country could support. Bayreuth, for example, a town with a population of 11,000, had some seventy-four master tailors, many of them starving for customers, all of them hurt. Complaints of this kind induced the government in 1834 to bring in still another law which restored to the guilds some of the monopolistic powers they had lost under the Montgelas regime. The law of 1834, in turn, raised a storm of protest, this time from consumers and from those who had entered trades without guild recognition. But their protests were powerless to effect any further change in Bavarian commercial law before 1848.

Elsewhere in Germany the guilds held firm. Of all the states, Baden had the best preserved guild system at this time.[20] Mecklenburg, Sachse-Weimar, and the four free

[19] August Popp, *Die Entstehung der Gewerbefreiheit in Bayern* (Leipzig, 1928), pp. 40–103; Gustav Schmoller, *Zur Geschichte der deutschen Kleingewerbe im neunzehnten Jahrhundert* (Halle, 1870), pp. 120–23.

[20] Bechtel, *Geschichte*, III, 214–19; Schmoller, *Kleingewerbe*, pp. 104–17, 140–47; Pierre Benaerts, *Les origines de la grande industrie allemande* (Paris, 1933), pp. 543–44; Paul Horster, *Die Entwicklung der saechsischen Gewerbeverfassung, 1780–1861* (Krefeld, 1908), pp. 35–66.

cities left guild privileges and monopolies almost untouched, while Hanover in 1815, Electoral Hesse in 1816,
and Oldenburg in 1830 reaffirmed guild regulations. In
Wuerttemberg, an ordinance of 1828 provided that factories could be opened by obtaining a simple license. But
apart from certain trades which lent themselves to factory
organization, guild control remained in full force. In Saxony, where the artisan class had been hard hit by the economic depression of the 1820's, a government official,
Eduard von Wietersheim, pointed the obvious moral that
the guild system could not guarantee a livelihood to guild
members. He proposed a gradual transition to *Gewerbefreiheit*, and after long discussion, and many false starts,
a law was enacted in 1840 which allowed free entry into
factory production and the building trades, and made licenses easier to get in rural districts.

Tracing the consequences of *Gewerbefreiheit* is difficult
because the guild members, particularly the masters who
had lost their privileges, tended to blame these reforms
for all the social and economic ills which beset them.[21] The
outcry began as early as the reforms themselves, rose in
a steady crescendo in the 1840's, and reached its climax in
the handworkers "parliaments" of 1848 at Hamburg early
in June and at Frankfurt am Main in midsummer. At
Frankfurt the guild masters, after excluding journeymen
from their sessions, drew up an "Artisans' Magna Charta"
which denounced *Gewerbefreiheit* in the name of a million
oppressed men. The lifting of guild regulations, they
claimed, had led to overcrowding of the trades. They demanded, therefore, a return to restrictions on the number
of master artisans in any given area and to compulsory
guild membership for all handworkers, including those
who worked in factories. *Gewerbefreiheit*, they believed,
had allowed new industries to spring up, industries which

---

[21] Benaerts, *Origines*, pp. 537–50; Rohrscheidt, *Zunftzwang*, pp. 558–
59; Schmoller, *Kleingewerbe*, pp. 83–86; Veit Valentin, *Geschichte der
deutschen Revolution von 1848–1849* (Berlin, 1930–31), II, 101–4.

were crushing the handicrafts. So they called for a ban on the introduction of new machinery and suggested the inhibition of the power-driven machines which were already in operation. Further, they demanded that only masters of guilds or corporations should be allowed to become proprietors of factories. These demands and grievances, taken at face value, have led some historians to dwell on the unfavorable effects of the liberal reforms and to present a picture of the 1840's as a period when large-scale industries began to flood the market with cheap goods, while hapless artisans, swarming together in the towns, bidding against each other for work, were reduced to destitution.[22]

"Certainly, distress has befallen the trades and handicrafts; but I ask is this distress any lighter where the guild system still exists?" This question raised in 1848 in the National Assembly at Frankfurt by an apologist for *Gewerbefreiheit* still deserves an answer.[23] It is true that not even well-preserved guild systems, such as those in Thuringia or Baden, could check the "flood of Prussian manufactured articles produced under a system of industrial freedom."[24] But surely the guild masters, where they retained power, could have restricted the admission of new members and thereby kept their trades from becoming overcrowded. Yet the influx of workers into the trades was greater in Baden where guild regulations remained in force than in Prussia where the dissolution of the guilds was most complete. Not all of the distress of the handicraftsmen, then, should be blamed on *Gewerbefreiheit*. Gustav Schmoller has pointed out that the sudden increase in the numbers of

[22] Juergen Kuczynski, *A Short History of Labour Conditions under Capitalism* (London, 1942–45), III, 26; Luetge, *Sozial- und Wirtschaftsgeschichte*, pp. 397–98; Hamerow, *Restoration, Revolution, Reaction*, pp. 30–31.

[23] Franz Wigard (ed.), *Stenographischer Bericht ueber die Verhandlungen der deutschen constituirenden Nationalversammlung zu Frankfurt am Main* (Leipzig, 1848–49), II, 855. The speaker was Georg Friedrich Kolb of the city of Speyer.

[24] Hamerow, *Restoration, Revolution, Reaction*, pp. 32–33.

artisans in the 1830's resulted from the fact that the trades were thriving rather than from the relaxation of guild restrictions. The hardships of the 1840's came about chiefly because a general business depression brought a sudden falling off in the demand for their services. No doubt the introduction of *Gewerbefreiheit* and the rise of factory industry harmed some handworkers, especially those in the textile and metal-smithing trades. But here again, it is pointless to exaggerate the harm done. Many trades, shoemaking, for example, had nothing whatever to fear from industrial competition at this time, while many others, particularly the building trades, positively benefited from industrial growth.[25]

No simple judgment can do justice to the record of the liberal reforms. The agrarian reforms improved the position of the peasants in many parts of southern and western Germany, whereas in the central and eastern provinces of Prussia the execution of these reforms brought hardship to hundreds of thousands. And although the guild masters' case against *Gewerbefreiheit* was naïve and overdrawn, the decline of guild controls in Prussia, Bavaria, and those areas formerly under French law did injure some artisans and caused anxiety to many more. But these reforms also had the long-term result of breaking down traditional rigidities in German society, so that it could meet the demands of a new age. The reforms encouraged greater productivity in both agriculture and manufacture by forcing individual producers to compete with each other and by enabling them to adopt new methods of production. And, in the long run, greater productivity was the best possible response to the challenge of population growth.

THE NEW TECHNOLOGIES

New and more efficient methods of soil care, planting, and stock-breeding, methods borrowed largely from English experience but adapted to German conditions, made

---

[25] Schmoller, *Kleingewerbe*, pp. 82–86, and *passim*.

their way into Germany in the early nineteenth century thanks to the work of Albrecht Thaer, Johann Schwerz, Johann Koppe, and a handful of their disciples.[26] One of the chief purposes of the liberal land reforms had been to induce farmers, in their own interests, to shift to these new methods. The pioneers of scientific agriculture, with projects for irrigation and drainage and recommendations for the use of fertilizers, did much to change the face of rural Germany. But the most sweeping change which these men brought about was the abandonment of the three-field system of planting in favor of systematic crop rotation which ended the wasteful practice of letting fields lie fallow.

That German farmers within the space of one generation were persuaded to break with age-old habits of work can be explained in part by the vigorous educational work of the reformers.[27] In 1806 Thaer founded an agricultural college at Moeglin, an estate in Brandenburg, and during the next few decades similar colleges were opened in Saxony, Wuerttemberg, Bavaria, Hesse, and in both the eastern and western provinces of Prussia. Enrollment at all of these schools was small, averaging between twenty and sixty students in each graduating class. But the importance of the schools can not be measured by their attendance figures. All the schools had estates attached to them which served as experimental stations and model farms where neighboring farmers could learn through observation. The colleges also held periodic exhibitions of farm products and farm tools, and sponsored competitions for prize livestock. The governments of Wuerttemberg and Bavaria op-

[26] Goltz, *Geschichte*, II, 3–83; Richard Krzymowski, *Geschichte der deutschen Landwirtschaft* (2d ed.; Stuttgart, 1951), pp. 210–18.

[27] Goltz, *Geschichte*, II, 127–31. Contemporary descriptions of the progress of agricultural science can be found in Karl Fraas, *Grundriss der Landwirtschaftslehre* (Stuttgart, 1848), pp. 67–77; Lengerke, *Statistik*, pp. 367–90; Charles Edouard Royer, *L'agriculture allemande, ses écoles, son organisation, ses moeurs, et ses pratiques les plus récentes* (Paris, 1847).

erated lower schools (*Ackerbauschulen*) for the training of fieldworkers. Still another agency of instruction was the agricultural society. During the 1830's and 1840's local societies multiplied throughout Germany and in 1837 their members met at the first Annual Congress of German Farmers. By 1848 the societies were active and numerous enough to maintain central offices in such cities as Berlin, Munich, Leipzig, Stuttgart, and Karlsruhe. These offices co-ordinated their work and facilitated the exchange of information.

German farmers were ready to learn from the agricultural colleges and societies because of the obvious advantages of the new methods which they taught. There was an immediate profit to be had by raising crops where in the fallow season none had grown before. Non-cereal crops which were alternated with cereals — crops such as tobacco, sugar beets, and oilseed — brought a cash return from the processing industries. Others, such as turnips, beets, and hay, were useful as animal fodder and enabled more farmers to keep livestock in stalls and, as a by-product, collect more manure for their fields. Finally, the soil, replenished by fertilizers and by careful selection of crops, produced more generous yields than ever before.[28]

Rapid progress was also made in animal husbandry. Throughout Germany, with the rising demand for meat and dairy products and for hides and wool, and with the growing supply of fodder, there was a sharp rise in the numbers of livestock. In Prussia between 1831 and 1849, the number of cattle increased by 20.8 per cent, sheep by 38.7 per cent, and swine by 42.0 per cent. Stock raisers

[28] The only challenge to Thaer's methods at this time came from Justus Liebig, a pioneer in soil chemistry, who claimed that Thaer's use of fertilizers was unscientific. But Thaer's defenders held the field, because, scientific or not, his methods brought better harvests. See Justus Liebig, *Die organische Chemie in ihrer Anwendung auf Agrikultur und Physiologie* (Brunswick, 1840); Friedrich Schulze-Gaevernitz, *Liebig oder Thaer* (Jena, 1846).

during this period also succeeded in raising healthier herds and in increasing the production of milk per cow. It has been estimated that between 1800 and 1850 the average weight of cattle increased by 30 to 40 per cent, with the consequence that whereas in 1805 a good cow was expected to give some 315 gallons of milk a year, in 1839 the expected yield was from 415 to 450 gallons.[29]

The adoption of more efficient farming methods raised German food production sufficiently to meet the demands of the growing population during the first half of the century. The improvement in the numbers and quality of livestock has already been noted. Meanwhile the division of commons and the abandonment of the three-field system increased the acreage under cultivation by at least 20 per cent.[30] Moreover, the average yield per acre increased. Statistics on crops are unavailable for any large area of Germany during the 1830's and 1840's. But by studying estimates and statistics for limited areas, the historian can arrive at an approximate index of the increase in food production. Using sources of this kind, a student working under the direction of Theodor von der Goltz consulted the estimates of Thaer in 1813 and of Koppe in 1845 to compare the yield per acre expected of different crops.[31] He discovered that between those years the expected yield of what increased 10.9 per cent, rye, 49.3 per cent, and barley, 25.8 per cent. Next, he compiled figures from detailed studies of the operation of twenty-six estates in Prussia and Saxony. These figures showed comparable increases in the actual yield per acre during the same period covered by Thaer's and Koppe's estimates. Finally, he showed that

[29] Goltz, *Geschichte*, II, 263–64; Peter Wagner, *Die Steigerung der Rohertraege in der Landwirtschaft im Laufe des neunzehnten Jahrhunderts* (Jena, 1896), p. 58; Joseph Bergfried Esslen, *Die Fleischversorgung des deutschen Reiches* (Stuttgart, 1912), pp. 241–44.

[30] Wagner, *Steigerung*, p. 30; Siegfried von Ciriacy-Wantrup, *Agrarkrisen und Stockungsspannen* (Berlin, 1936), p. 42.

[31] Wagner, *Steigerung*, *passim*.

until 1870 German grain exports exceeded grain imports and thus argued that until that date the increase in food production outstripped population growth.

Taking into account these estimates and the fact that the number of acres under tillage increased, Theodor von der Goltz concluded that between 1800 and 1850 the productivity of German agriculture increased by an average of 50 per cent. His conclusion remains open to question.[32] The estimates of Koppe and Thaer, and the statistics of the twenty-six estates studied, are based almost entirely on observation of harvests on large estates where farming was likely to be more efficient than on small farms. Moreover, the presence of an exportable grain surplus despite population growth proves very little unless accompanied by evidence that the annual consumption of grain per person either rose or remained constant. Despite such reservations concerning a 50 per cent increase in food production, it is probably safe to conclude that the rising curve of productivity did keep up with the population curve which rose 38.7 per cent between 1816 and 1846.

German industrialists, like German agriculturalists, learned from British masters and British models.[33] Late in the eighteenth century, machines, made in England, were imported to Germany. They were followed by British experts and entrepreneurs, who, like the Cockerill brothers established new industries in Germany, and by British mechanics who helped to organize production. Germans crossed the Channel on official and unofficial visits to observe new methods of production and to confer with manufacturers. Count Friedrich Wilhelm von Reden, for

[32] Goltz, *Geschichte*, II, 268; Erich Jordan, *Die Entstehung der konservativen Partei und die presussischen Agrarverhaeltnisse* (Munich, 1914), p. 41.

[33] W. O. Henderson, *Britain and Industrial Europe, 1750–1870* (Liverpool, 1954), pp. 139–66; Franz Schnabel, *Deutsche Geschichte im neunzehnten Jahrhundert* (Freiburg im Breisgau, 1929–36), III, 262–330; Thomas Charles Banfield, *Industry of the Rhine, Series II: Manufactures* (London, 1848), p. 222.

example, head of the Bureau of Mines for Silesia, went to England on an official visit to observe new smelting processes in 1776; but many Germans, for example, Alfred Krupp during 1838 and 1839, traveled there in their own private interests. German governments not only subsidized the travel of English experts to Germany, and of German experts to Britain, they began to found schools to instruct their citizens in new methods of production. During the 1820's, schools of engineering were opened in Karlsruhe, Munich, Nuernberg, Dresden, Hanover, and Darmstadt. The *Gewerbeinstitut*, founded at Berlin in 1821, combined the functions of an engineering college with those of a government commission for industrial development. German educators in the 1820's also began to set up trade schools, and by the 1840's Germany had the nucleus of a trained labor force.

The change from old to new methods of production in Germany, as elsewhere, began early in the textile industry and made most rapid progress in those branches of the industry which had the most favorable market conditions.[34] In the 1820's and 1830's, a drastic fall in the price of raw cotton made cotton cloth the cheapest and most commonly used material in Germany. By 1849 the average consumer in Prussia was annually using sixteen ells of cotton cloth as against five ells of linen and only one ell of woolen cloth. Machines for spinning cotton yarn were brought to Germany as early as 1783 and under the Continental System a great many spinning mills using water power were established in the Sieg, Wupper, and Ruhr valleys. The sharp rise in demand for cotton goods which began in the 1820's encouraged mechanization. By the mid-1840's, the German Customs Union (*Zollverein*) had some 300 cotton-spinning mills, which were operating some 750,300 spindles. As cotton goods gained in popularity, the market for linen de-

[34] Benaerts, *Origines*, pp. 379–87, pp. 475–88; Schmoller, *Kleingewerbe*, pp. 453–575; Friedrich Otto Dilthey, *Die Geschichte der niederrheinischen Baumwollindustrie* (Jena, 1908), pp. 1–11.

clined. In 1843 the Zollverein had only twenty mills with 26,000 spindles producing linen yarn. Cloth-weaving was much slower to mechanize than spinning. In 1846, for the production of cotton, linen, wool, and silk cloth, the Zollverein had 7,750 mechanical looms, as opposed to 99,800 hand looms. Weaving, then, was still very much a "domestic" industry in which the weavers worked at home for entrepreneurs who supplied them with yarn and paid them for the finished cloth.

New processes of smelting ore and of puddling iron to make steel had only begun to transform the German metallurgical industry before 1850.[35] Pig iron smelted in coke furnaces accounted for 4.5 per cent of the total production in the Zollverein in 1834, and for 10.8 per cent in 1850. The first coke furnace in Germany was built at Gleiwitz in Upper Silesia as early as 1794. But as late as 1848, of the seventy-six smelting furnaces in that district (*Regierungsbezirk* Oppeln), sixty still burned wood fuel. Progress in western Germany was even slower. The first coke furnaces there were built in the Saar basin in the 1820's; the Ruhr district had none until the late 1840's. Gradually, however, the iron industry was moving away from the old centers of production in mountainous areas, where wood fuel was plentiful, down to the coal basins. Partly for that reason, and partly because of the exhaustion of local ore deposits, the Thueringenwald, the Frankenwald, the Erzgebirge, and the Siegerland began to decline as centers of iron production. Between 1836 and 1849 the number of ironworks in the Siegerland fell off from 383 to 259.

Because water-power was abundant and capital was scarce in Germany, manufacturers were slow to invest in

[35] Benaerts, *Origines*, pp. 447–59; Ludwig Beck, *Die Geschichte des Eisen* (Brunswick, 1884–1903), IV, 175–87; Otto Johannsen, *Geschichte des Eisens* (Dusseldorf, 1925), pp. 145–58; Johannes Mueller, *Die Industrialisierung der deutschen Mittelgebirge* (Jena, 1938), pp. 4–34; Kurt Wiedenfeld, *Ein Jahrhundert rheinischer Montan-industrie, 1815–1915* (Bonn, 1916), pp. 10–11.

steam-engines to drive their machinery.[36] In the 1780's engines built in England, or in Germany from English designs, had been put to work in mining operations. But in 1837 Prussia still had only 419 steam engines, a number which in the next twelve years rose to 1,582, not counting locomotives and marine engines. All the other states lagged behind Prussia in this respect. Saxony, the most thoroughly industrialized state in Germany, had only 233 steam engines in 1846; Bavaria had 49; and Baden had 24. Most of these engines were small, with an average output of from fifteen to twenty-five horsepower. As T. C. Banfield observed in the mid-1840's, it took a very serious drought to teach German industrialists the merits of steam.

In the whole Prussian dominions the engines driving mills for spinning or weaving amounted but to 215, of 2,981.5 horsepower, not much exceeding fourteen horsepower on the average. Frequent and no doubt skilful use is often made of water-power in factories, and we have pointed out numerous instances where this is done. But the precarious nature of water-power does not suit a period of brisk competition. . . . In 1846, the hot summer put a stop to nearly all operations that depended on water-power, even to navigation on smaller rivers. The long winter that succeeded condemned all water-wheels to inaction until late in the spring. It is this clinging to the old accustomed dependence . . . that constitutes the difficulty of the state of transition through which Germany is progressing.[37]

One of the most significant developments in the history of industrialization in Germany was the growth of a machine-making industry in the first half of the nineteenth century.[38] Because of their dependence on imported British

[36] Benaerts, Origines, p. 376; Otto Froriep, *Zur Geschichte der Maschinenbau- industrie und der Maschinenzoelle im deutschen Zollverein* (Stuttgart, 1918), p. 33; Conrad Matschoss, *Die Entwicklung der Dampfmaschine* (Berlin, 1908), I, 140–207.

[37] Banfield, *Manufactures*, p. 234.

[38] Froriep, *Maschinenbau-industrie*, pp. 14–44; Fritz Redlich, "Leaders of the German Steam Engine Industry during the First Hundred Years," *Journal of Economic History*, IV (1944), 121–48.

and Belgian machines, the German states did not give tariff protection to German firms which pioneered in machine manufacturing until 1844. Nevertheless, owing to the foresight of a small number of entrepreneurs, the Zollverein in 1846 had 434 machine-making plants with some 13,232 workers and was increasingly able to supply the demand in Germany. Between 1840 and 1844, for instance, German locomotive manufacturers could supply only 18 per cent of the locomotives needed in the Zollverein. Between 1845 and 1850, they were able to supply 79 per cent.

The use of expensive machinery in textile manufacturing and of complicated new processes in the iron industry meant the beginnings of the factory system in Germany.[39] However, the concentration of production in large firms was not very far advanced before 1850. A few of the heavy industries employed several hundred workers. In the 1840's, for instance, the Gute Hoffnungshuette employed between 500 and 600 workers; the Laurahuette in Silesia employed some 700. But these were exceptions. As late as 1849, the average number of workers in heavy industries in Prussia and Saxony was twenty-five. Prussian cotton-spinning mills employed an average of thirty-four workers, and in the spinning mills of Saxony the average work force was sixty-three.

Although Germany had begun to feel some of the short-term disadvantages of industrialization, such as technological unemployment among the artisans, industries had not grown enough before 1850 to make the advantages of the new system apparent. New production methods had increased the output of both heavy and light goods somewhat but not enough to provide consumers with an abundance of inexpensive goods.[40] If we let the production figures

[39] Werner Sombart *Die Deutsche Volkswirtschaft im neunzehnten Jahrhundert* (7th ed.; Berlin, 1927), pp. 298–314; Hans Ehrenberg, *Die Eisenhuettentechnik und der deutsche Huettenarbeiter* (Stuttgart, 1906), pp. 43–55; Benaerts, *Origines*, pp. 495–99.

[40] Kuczynski, *Labour Conditions*, III, 16–17; Froriep, *Maschinenbauindustrie*, pp. 30–31.

for 1860 (after the great expansion of the 1850's) equal 100, the index of pig iron production in the Zollverein will be seen to have risen from twenty-seven in the period 1836–39 to forty in the period 1844–47, and the index of production of cotton goods, from twenty-six to forty-two. Nor had the new industries grown fast enough to absorb manpower from those areas which suffered from overpopulation. For every ten thousand people in the Zollverein in 1847, only twenty worked in spinning mills, only eleven in ironworks, and only four in machine-making industries. The sluggish pace of industrial growth before 1850, rather than industrialization itself, was responsible for much of the social distress of the 1840's. And the reasons why industrial development was so slow in coming must be sought in the backward state of the German market, which in the early nineteenth century had only begun to break with its medieval past.

THE STATE OF THE MARKET

At the turn of the century small producers still sold to small, local markets. Weak and divided politically, the German states built customs barriers against each other, confused trade by maintaining a variety of currencies, held jealously to their privileges to interrupt river traffic, and had no plans for highway communications which reached beyond their own frontiers. The state of the German market can be seen very clearly in the story of a transaction which took place in 1818 when the Royal Prussian Iron Foundry at Gleiwitz in Upper Silesia built a steam engine for a mine company in the Saar district. The engine had to be shipped by waterways on a roundabout journey which involved transshipment at Hamburg, Amsterdam, Cologne, Koblenz, and Trier, lasted four and one-half months, and added 26 per cent to the purchase price of the machine in the form of customs duties which were levied by weight.[41] In

---

[41] Froriep, *Maschinenbau-industrie*, p. 9; for a brief description of market conditions, see W. O. Henderson, *The Zollverein* (Cambridge, 1939), pp. 1–20; Benaerts, *Origines*, pp. 15–58.

their trade relations with other countries the German states had very little bargaining power to force reciprocal concessions. And in a country which had been commercially backward since the sixteenth century, there were few great mercantile fortunes which could provide, as they did in Britain, investment capital for the development of the economy.

Many German states after 1815 experimented with tariff reform. A notably successful experiment was the Prussian tariff of 1818, which combined a policy of moderate protection for the home market with provisions for free exchange within that market.[42] The failure of the Germanic Confederation to eliminate trade barriers within its borders and Prussia's seizure of the initiative after 1820 in forming a customs union within the Confederation were events of long-range political and economic importance. By 1836, the German Customs Union, or Zollverein, had, in effect, extended the Prussian tariff of 1818 to all the German states with the exception of Austria, the seaports of Hamburg, Bremen, and Luebeck, and a small cluster of states in the northwest which included Hanover, Brunswick, Oldenburg, and the two Mecklenburgs. The Zollverein brought some immediate benefits to German commerce. It created an unrestricted market for some twenty-five million consumers, and it led directly to further institutional reforms. For example, the member states met at a currency convention in Dresden in 1838 and took some first steps toward unifying their monetary systems. But the importance of these immediate benefits should not be exaggerated. Referring to the formation of the Zollverein and the currency agreement of 1838, Joseph Schumpeter noted:

[42] The text of the Prussian tariff of 1818 is in Wilifried von Eisenhart Rothe and A. Ritthaler (eds.), *Vorgeschichte und Begruendung des deutschen Zollvereins, 1815–1834* (Berlin, 1934), I, 71–78. For events leading to formation of the Zollverein, see Henderson, *Zollverein,* pp. 21–127; W. Weber, *Der deutsche Zollverein* (2d ed.; Leipzig, 1871), pp. 84–300; Arnold H. Price, *The Evolution of the Zollverein* (Ann Arbor, Mich., 1949).

They undoubtedly conditioned both enterprise and growth ever after, although they asserted themselves but slowly in the course of the century. What they immediately accomplished was only removal of fetters from the things initiated in, and crippled by, these fetters.[43]

The flow of goods between members of the Zollverein was just beginning during the 1840's. One of the arguments which promoters of the union had used in negotiations for its formation, indeed the classical argument of free traders everywhere, was that the abolition of customs barriers would encourage each district to specialize in producing whatever it could produce best. The southern states, while dickering over entry into the Zollverein, had been particularly interested in the prospect of selling their agricultural produce to the northern states which had more highly developed industries.[44] Some such exchange did begin after union. The Rhineland bought grain from Bavaria and Wuerttemberg as well as from the eastern provinces of Prussia. Some northern weavers bought yarn from southern spinning mills. Saxony, with its large population and many centers of industry, began to bring in food from other German states. But the volume of such trade was not heavy. As late as the 1860's, Saxony was annually importing only three weeks' supply of grain.[45] A British observer who visited Germany just before 1850 pointed out that the tradition of local self-sufficiency died hard.

The German league comprehends above twenty-six millions of

[43] Joseph A. Schumpeter, *Business Cycles* (New York, 1939), I, 280, n.1.

[44] Karl Friedrich Nebenius, *Der deutsche Zollverein, sein System und seine Zukunft* (Karlsruhe, 1835), pp. 101–22; Eisenhart Rothe and Ritthaler (eds.), *Vorgeschichte*, II, 24, 41, 123. On the immediate consequences of union for German trade, see Wilhelm Thieme, *Eintritt Sachsens in den Zollverein und seine wirtschaftlichen Folgen* (Leipzig, 1914), pp. 85–96; Banfield, *Agriculture*, p. 24; John Bowring, "Report on Prussian Trade for Her Majesty's Government," *Parliamentary Papers*, 1840, XXI, 33, 60; Émile Jacquemin, *L'Allemagne agricole, industrielle et politique* (Paris, 1842), p. 34.

[45] Georg von Viebahn, *Statistik des zollvereinten und noerdlichen Deutschlands* (Berlin, 1858–68), II, 951.

people; and if we only look at the numbers and at the extent and fertility of the soil they occupy, they should be buyers in their home market of manufacturing industry, one would suppose, as extensively at least as our British twenty-four millions. But here we see the immense difference produced by a different social economy. These twenty-six millions consume less of each other's industry, employ less, buy less, sell less, than four millions of our population. In our social system every man buys all he uses, and sells all he produces; there is a perpetual exchange of industry for industry.[46]

In the 1840's the Zollverein also began to give German producers some protection against foreign competition.[47] The Prussian tariff of 1818 had imposed light duties on imported finished products but had left industrial materials, such as raw cotton, wool, ores, and chemicals, either duty-free or almost so. This policy, extended to the entire Zollverein, seemed to be satisfactory until the 1840's when the proprietors of spinning mills and iron works demanded protection against imported British yarn and pig iron. Their demands were resisted by finishing industries which wanted to go on buying British imports which were cheaper than the German products, and often of superior quality. Protectionist demands were opposed also by Prussian agricultural interests which feared that exclusion of British articles from the Zollverein might lead to the exclusion of Prussian grain from the British market. The issue was joined at the Zollverein congresses of 1842, 1843, and 1845, with the representatives Baden and Wuerttemberg leading the fight for protection and the Prussians leading the opposition. In 1842, German iron manufacturers were conceded some slight tariff protection. In 1846, after Saxony and Bavaria had joined Baden and Wuerttemberg in their demands, and after repeal of the Corn Laws in Britain seemed to assure the Prussian grain interests of an open

[46] Samuel Laing, *Notes of a Traveller* (2d ed.; Philadelphia, 1846), p. 152.

[47] Beck, *Geschichte*, IV, 695; Benaerts, *Origines*, pp. 215–44; Dilthey, *Baumwollindustrie*, pp. 18–22; Henderson, *Zollverein*, pp. 179–89.

market, the German spinning industries were granted low tariffs on imported yarn.

The Zollverein improved to some extent the German's bargaining power in their trade relations with other countries.[48] In the 1830's, the officials of the Zollverein met British demands for the lowering of import duties on manufactures and colonial produce with counterdemands for the reduction of British duties on German grain and timber. Hardly decisive in the parliamentary struggle which developed over the repeal of the Corn Laws, this German pressure did provide advocates of repeal with arguments which were declaimed in public and were written into the petition drafted for presentation to Parliament in September, 1838, by the Anti-Corn Law Association (later, League). At the urging of the southern German states, similar pressure was brought to bear on France in the 1840's. In 1842 the Zollverein congress threatened to double import duties on French articles such as gloves and cognac unless France lowered her duties on German exports such as wool and cattle. The French government yielded and reduced some duties. A commercial treaty between Belgium and the Zollverein in 1844 maintained free transit rights for German shippers on the Antwerp-Cologne railway but only at the cost of giving Belgian iron exporters a preferential tariff rate in the German market. Although these quite modest gains were achieved, the Zollverein failed altogether in some trade negotiations. The Danes could not be persuaded to reduce sound dues for German shipping, and the Dutch refused to lower their toll charges on Rhine River traffic. Meanwhile both Austria and Russia preserved high tariff walls against German manufactures, although Russia in 1844 did make some concessions to German silk, wool, and iron imports.

[48] Henderson, *Zollverein*, pp. 127–38; Bowring, "Report," pp. 50–59; Archibald Prentice, *History of the Anti-Corn-Law League* (London, 1853), I, 64–66; Werner Thiedig, *Englands Uebergang zum Freihandel und die deutsche Handelspolitik, 1840–1846* (Giessen, 1927).

What little the Zollverein did to strengthen Germany's position in foreign markets worked to the advantage of the agricultural interests.[49] During the 1840's, a general expansion of the export market for German farm products forecast the era of great agricultural prosperity after 1850. This expansion resulted in part from the greater leverage that the Zollverein gave German exporters in international trade, but a more fundamental reason for it was the lack of much trans-Atlantic competition in supplying food to industrial England and, increasingly, to Belgium. Not until the period between 1839 and 1842 did Britain import any large quantities of grain from North America and then only as a result of an unusually high demand. In the years 1843 to 1845, when the demand fell off, Britain bought 75 per cent of its grain imports from Germany. The average annual export of grain from Germany in the years between 1846 and 1850 was 22 per cent higher than in the period between 1841 and 1845. Through the entire decade of the 1840's, the average annual export of farm products other than grain and cattle was 27 per cent higher than during the period between 1836 and 1840. Meanwhile the Zollverein's grudging concessions to the demands of German industrialists for tariff protection actually left the market open to foreign articles. Between 1836 and 1840, foreign spinning mills supplied 70 per cent of the yarn used in the German textile industry. Even after the tariff revision of 1846, they kept 65 per cent of the market. In 1843 the Zollverein imported some 53 per cent of its pig iron, and in 1850 they still depended on Belgian and English producers for 35 per cent.

The comparatively rapid improvement of Germany's transportation network between 1820 and 1840 probably

[49] Johann Richard Mucke, *Deutschlands Getreideverkehr mit dem Auslande* (Greifswald, 1887), pp. 218–64; Gertrud Hermes, "Statistische Studien zum zollvereinten Deutschland," *Archiv fuer Sozialwissenschaft und Sozialpolitik*, LXIII (1930), 123–30; Benaerts, *Origines*, pp. 460–61, p. 489.

brought more immediate benefits to German commerce than did the foundation of the Zollverein.[50] In Germany, as in the United States at that time, waterways carried most of the freight and did so with increasing efficiency. According to Article 19 of the Federal Constitution of June 8, 1815, the Germanic Confederation undertook to open Germany's great river system to free navigation. The actual working out of details among the riparian states took time, especially in those cases in which the consent of non-German states such as France or Holland was necessary. A treaty freeing navigation on the Elbe was signed in 1821, another for the Weser in 1823, and another for the Rhine in 1831. Meanwhile other treaties opened up tributary streams like the Neckar, the Main, and the Lahn. These treaties enabled the various states to abolish such medieval obstacles to shipping as staple rights and transfer rights. They abolished the restrictive guilds of boatmen and set up commissions to supervise river traffic and recommend improvements in port facilities, towpaths, and the like. While it proved impossible to do away entirely with river tolls, the lifting of other restrictions brought on a tremendous expansion of river trade.

The advent of steam navigation in the 1830's made river shipping cheaper and more dependable. At first, steamships were used almost exclusively for passenger service. But within a few years shippers proved that the use of a steam tug to pull several freight barges was a much more efficient means of transport than that provided by boatmen with their horse relays. In 1844 nearly 80 per cent of river freight was still carried in sailboats or horse-drawn barges. In 1847 50 per cent of it was carried in barges towed by

[50] Schumpeter, *Cycles*, I, 280, n.1; Banfield, *Manufactures*, pp. 188–89; Meitzen, *Boden*, III, 247–48, 262; Edwin J. Clapp, *The Navigable Rhine* (Boston, 1907), pp. 11–19; Christian Eckert, *Rheinschiffahrt im neunzehnten Jahrhundert* (Leipzig, 1900), pp. 219–43; Kurt Fischer, *Eine Studie ueber die Elbschiffahrt* (Jena, 1907), pp. 1–16.

steam tugs.[51] Another boon to water transportation at this time was the extension of the canal system not only in Germany but throughout Europe. Enlightened rulers in the eighteenth century had already supplied Germany with a number of canals, which had only to be improved and lengthened in the early part of the nineteenth century. For example, the Klodnitz Canal in Upper Silesia, which was dug between 1788 and 1806, was extended in 1830, so that heavy barges could move from Gleiwitz to the Oder River. In 1836 the German states had some 337 miles of canals, and between 1836 and 1847, an additional 134 miles were completed.

Overland transportation improved slowly in the early nineteenth century.[52] Plans of Friedrich von Motz, the Prussian Finance Minister in the 1820's, for a rational highway system connecting Prussia with the southern states became snarled in the political jealousies of the Germanic Confederation. Still, between 1816 and 1842 the mileage of highways within Prussia quadrupled, and other states began to follow Prussia's example. Railroads, meanwhile, were regarded as novelties for the rapid transportation of passengers until, gradually, in the 1840's German shippers began to see the advantages of rail transportation over horse-drawn wagons. Between 1844 and 1847 the tonnage of freight shipment by rail in Prussia increased threefold. By 1847 a railway net was beginning to take shape with 1,598 miles of track in use and an additional 2,935 miles under construction. Although German railroad builders could not get all the capital they wanted as quickly as they wanted it, they managed, according to one estimate, to

[51] Meitzen, *Boden*, III, 262; Richard Eger, *Die Binnenschiffahrt in Europa und Nordamerika* (Berlin, 1899), p. 11.

[52] Paul Thimme, *Strassenbau und Strassenpolitik in Deutschland zur Zeit der Gruendung des Zollvereins* (Stuttgart, 1931), p. 80; Meitzen, *Boden*, III, 232; Bowring, "Report," pp. 7, 10–11; Benaerts, *Origines*, pp. 291–329; Kuczynski, *Labour Conditions*, III, 17; Joseph Hansen, *Gustav von Mevissen, ein rheinisches Lebensbild, 1815–1899* (Berlin, 1906), I, 427–28.

draw an average of 100 million marks into their companies each year between 1842 and 1847. For Germany, this involved a heavy commitment of capital to an enterprise which, until the great trunk lines were connected in the 1850's, could not begin to repay its cost.

The financing of railroad construction, like the financing of industrial development generally, was complicated by the peculiarities of the German money market. The country's resources of capital were dispersed among a large number of relatively small holders who preferred government bonds to any other form of investment. Industrial entrepreneurs had the problem of calling some of this capital into more productive use. The formation of joint-stock companies was not a particularly happy solution since stock issues in the 1840's seemed to attract speculators looking for quick profits rather than long-term investors. Industrialists, especially in the early years of their companies' growth, needed more solid financial backing than that supplied by shareholders who began to unload their holdings at the least tremor in public confidence.[53]

Quite possibly, capital for the development of new industrial enterprises was difficult to get because German society in the early nineteenth century was still tradition-bound. Many of the early entrepreneurs came from artisan families; they brought no large personal fortunes into their businesses and were often incapable of inspiring trust among the wealthier classes. Many potential investors, reared with a genteel contempt for business and businessmen, preferred buying land or government securities to risking their money on industrial shares.[54] Social prestige was not to be won by becoming part-owner of a textile mill;

[53] Hanns Leiskow, *Spekulation und oeffentliche Meinung in der ersten Haelfte des neunzehnten Jahrhunderts* (Jena, 1930), pp. 1–15; Adolf Weber, *Depositenbanken und Spekulationsbanken* (2d ed.; Munich, 1915), pp. 59–63.

[54] On the humble origins of the entrepreneurs, see Schnabel, *Deutsche Geschichte*, III, 436–37; the disdain of the upper classes for business enterprise is discussed in Sombart, *Deutsche Volkswirtschaft*, pp. 464–66.

but considerable amounts of money could be lost. It is significant that in November, 1842, when the government of Prussia eliminated risk in the purchase of railway stocks by guaranteeing a certain minimum return, there was a headlong rush of investors into that market.

What the industrialist needed but could not get was bank credit. Both the Prussian and Bavarian governments maintained semi-official banks authorized to take deposits and to help landowners and merchants over periods of crisis with short-term loans. But they were not investment banks. Private banking houses, meanwhile, were reluctant to tie up large sums of money in new-fangled ventures. Of the thirty major banking houses in Berlin at this time, not one would advance any substantial amount of money for industrial development. Bankers in Cologne and Breslau, who were much closer to the areas of potential development, were only a few degrees less cautious. The problem was eventually solved by the establishment of credit banks. The first of these was chartered in 1848 when the A. Schaafhausen'scher Bankverein of Cologne was founded on the ruins of a private bank that had been destroyed by the crisis of the late 1840's. But the movement of credit banks into the general money market did not make much headway until the founding of the Bank fuer Handel und Industrie in Darmstadt in 1853.[55]

Economic change in Germany before 1848, then, heralded the beginnings of a modern, dynamic economy. Liberal reforms, where they were enacted, allowed the economy to adapt itself more readily to the demands of a new age, particularly to the demands set up by rapid population growth. Increased productivity in agriculture, an indispensable condition for economic growth, was the clearest net gain of the period. Industrial development, on the other hand, might have been more rapid if German businessmen had moved more quickly to seize the oppor-

[55] Bechtel, *Wirtschaftsgeschichte*, III, 181; Benaerts, *Origines*, pp. 273–82.

tunities created by the Zollverein and by improved methods of transportation, and if they had succeeded earlier in finding a means for the effective mobilization of capital. Nevertheless, industries had begun to develop and conditions had begun to improve by the 1840's. Wilhelm Dieterici, the Prussian statistician cited earlier in this chapter, had reason for optimism when in 1846 he said that during the preceding decades Germans had passed from circumstances of poverty, necessity, and privation to a life of material comfort; that "living standards have improved continuously over a period of years, and unless all observations are misleading, they are bound to go on improving."[56]

Dieterici's confidence seems to have been proven false, however, by the massive evidence of social distress in the 1840's. At the same time that this government statistician could point to gains already made and make cheerful predictions of greater gains to come, other observers were producing "a flood of writings on the general distress, the social problem, and the working-class movement."[57] One explanation for these contradictions is, of course, that many of the economic gains which Dieterici registered in his statistics were made at the expense of certain classes of artisans and peasants. Another explanation is that population increases together with the "throw-off" of labor which resulted from land reforms and innovations in manufacturing had created a surplus of workers while industrial development and general economic growth had been too slow to absorb this surplus. Finally, it should be emphasized that much of the distress of the 1840's was quite local and temporary in character, a fact which will emerge from a closer examination of the social conditions at that time.

[56] Dieterici, *Volkswohlstand*, p. xvii.

[57] The phrase is taken from a lengthy, but still far from exhaustive bibliographical review of such writing: Paul Mombert, "Aus der Literatur ueber die soziale Frage und ueber die Arbeiterbewegung in Deutschland in der ersten Haelfte des neunzehnten Jahrhunderts," *Archiv fuer Gechichte des Sozialismus und der Arbeiterbegwegung*, IX (1921), 169–236.

II

Social Conditions

There is a striking contradiction between statistical evidence of economic progress and literary evidence of social distress in Germany during the 1830's and 1840's. To resolve the contradiction, it should be borne in mind that while literature is always an invaluable source for tracing changes in tastes and opinions and states of mind it is not always a dependable source for the study of actual social conditions.[1] German writers of the 1830's had not yet broken out of the spell which the romantics of an earlier generation had cast upon their countrymen. Realism came into vogue only after 1850. The "Young Germans" of the prerevolutionary period, writers such as Heinrich Heine, Karl Gutzkow, and Heinrich Laube, became passionately interested in the causes of religious freedom, Polish independence, and, under Saint-Simonian influence, the "rehabilitation of the flesh." But they rarely wrote about the lives of ordinary people, and when they did, they wrote in a lyrical-pastoral vein. Heine, for instance, in his *Reisebilder* (1826–27) left us an idyllic sketch of a mining community in the Harz Mountains. Laube's *Reisenovellen* (1834–37) which is a

---

[1] For literary trends during this period, see Hugo Bieber, *Der Kampf um die Tradition* (Stuttgart, 1928), pp. 63–221. For works on the Young Germans, see E. M. Butler, *The Saint-Simonian Religion in Germany* (Cambridge, 1926); on Buechner, see Karl Viëtor, *Georg Buechner* (Bern, 1949), pp. 72–92, and A. J. H. Knight, *Georg Buechner* (Oxford, 1951), pp. 34–40; on Immermann, see Ernst Kohn-Bramstedt, *Aristocracy and Middle Class in Germany* (London, 1937), pp. 44–67.

dull and often ludicrous imitation of Heine, has scenes set in Silesia where the author's only comment on the peasants is to remark that they lack imagination.

One of the most original writers of the period, Georg Buechner, showed considerable understanding of the lower classes in his dramatic works but made no attempt to describe their material circumstances with the exception of a few lines about the hard lot of the Hessian peasants in his revolutionary pamphlet, *Der hessische Landbote* (1834). Ida, Countess von Hahn-Hahn, a writer who was known as "the George Sand of Germany," presumably because she wore trousers and advocated easy divorce, showed none of George Sand's social sympathies. The plots of Countess Hahn-Hahn's novels are only enacted in fashionable drawing rooms and boudoirs. Just a shade less aristocratic in tone were the novels of an official of the Prussian judiciary, Karl Lebrecht Immermann. His *Die Epigonen* (1836), which portrayed the struggle between the grasping industrial middle class of Westphalia and its rather effete aristocracy, merely hints at the unwholesome effects of factory life on the working class. His *Muenchhausen* (1838), an uncanny mixture of whimsy and satire, has one passage, called "Der Oberhof," which presents a highly idealized picture of rustic simplicity and virtue and leads up to a message of romantic agrarian conservatism very much like the contemporary views of Benjamin Disraeli, Lord John Manners, and the "Young England" set.

A taste for realism was quickened in Germany in the late 1830's and early 1840's by the translation of foreign authors, particularly of Charles Dickens and Eugène Sue.[2] Within eight years of the publication of *Pickwick Papers* (1836–37), all of Dickens's works up to that time had been

[2] Lawrence Marsden Price, *English Literature in Germany* (Berkeley, 1953), pp. 345–50; Ellis N. Gummer, *Dickens' Works in Germany, 1837–1937* (Oxford, 1940), pp. 10–36, 55–65; Erich Edler, *Eugène Sue und die deutsche Mysterienliteratur* (Berlin, 1932), pp. 17–47; J. Dresch, *Le roman social en Allemagne, 1850–1900* (Paris, 1913), pp. 4–21.

given at least three translations into German. Meanwhile imitations began to appear. Ferdinand Stolle's *Deutsche Pickwickier* (1841) presented good-natured scenes of Berlin street life and despite its literary shortcomings enjoyed considerable popularity. A piece of hack work, *Geheimnisse Londons, Englands und der Englaender* (1844), a compilation of scenes of vice and crime from Dickens's novels, borrowed its title from Sue's *Les mystères de Paris*. The latter appeared serially in France in 1843, was immediately translated into German, and spread across Europe a contagion of interest in the life of the underworld. In 1844 some thirty-six German cities from Berlin and Hamburg to Altenburg and Hildesheim had their mysteries revealed to a public with an apparently insatiable appetite for stories of poverty, murder, prostitution, and unnatural vice. Nearly all of the mystagogues moralized on poverty as the breeding ground of vice, but few of them had social reform as their primary interest. Certainly their overwrought pictures of urban squalor should be taken as reflecting the vagaries of public taste rather than actual social conditions.

Similar reservations must be made about the spate of poems, novels, and stories which appeared just before and after the tragic uprising of the Silesian weavers in June, 1844.[3] Public sympathy for the weavers and justifiable anger at the blundering of the governments in Berlin and Breslau ran high in the mid-1840's and found expression in verses like Heine's *Die schlesische Weber* (1845) and Ernst Dronke's *Das Weib des Webers* (1845). But a number of writers attempted to exploit both the public's interest in the weavers and the public's taste for the sensational. Louise Otto in *Schloss und Fabrik* (1846) and Otto Ruppius in *Eine Weberfamilie* (1846) gave reasonably honest descriptions of the hunger, the cold, the disease,

[3] Solomon Liptzin, *The Weavers in German Literature* (Baltimore, 1926), pp. 27–65. For the effects of this literature on public opinion, see Alfred Zimmermann, *Bluethe und Verfall des Leinengewerbes in Schlesien* (2d ed.; Leipzig, 1893), pp. 340–44.

and, worst of all, the deliberate abuse of the weavers. But others, like Ernst Willkomm in his story *Der Lohnweber* (1845) and Alexander von Ungern-Sternberg in his *Paul* (1845) catered to a taste for lurid incidents with accounts of suicide and the murdering of children by their desperate parents. In another of Willkomm's works, *Weisse Sklaven* (1845), two brothers, one a factory owner, the other a champion of the workers, fight a duel by operating a spinning machine. Shortly after the duel begins, the villainous factory owner is caught up in the machinery and scalped.

Not all of the literature of social protest was directed against employers. The radical poet Ferdinand Freiligrath, for example, predicted that social distress would lead directly to the overthrow of royal governments. Freiligrath made this prediction in the poem "Wie man's macht!" which he published in 1846 in a small collection of his work entitled *Ça ira*. The opening lines of the poem state that the people are hungry and cold and badly clothed. The poet goes on to imagine how a bold young man might lead the people in a raid on a military supply depot. After breaking into the army stores and sharing out the warm clothing which they find piled there, the people must face the anger of the military commanders who order their troops to open fire and charge the mob. But the soldiers answer, "We too are the people!" and refuse their orders. This local uprising then becomes a general revolution which sweeps into royal capitals, toppling thrones and smashing crowns. The closing lines of the poem predict that, sooner than men think, the downtrodden will rise amid fire and bloodshed to victory, and labor pains will end in the act of birth.[4] Freili-

---

[4] The opening and closing lines paraphrased above are: So wird es kommen, eh' ihr denkt: — Das Volk hat nicht zu beissen mehr! / Durch seine Lumpen pfeift der Wind! Wo nimmt es Brot und Kleider her? / . . . Aus Brand und Blut erhebt das Volk sieghaft sein lang zertreten Haupt / Wehen hat jegliche Geburt! — So wird es kommen, eh' irh glaubt!" See Paul Zaunert (ed.), *Freiligraths Werke* (Leipzig, 1912), I, 361–64. *Ça ira* was originally published in Switzerland, where Freiligrath lived in exile.

grath's rhetoric expresses one of the moods of the time. But the historian still wants to know just how bad conditions were. How widespread were the hunger and distress which aroused the poet's indignation?

Of considerably greater value as a social document is *Dies Buch gehoert dem Koenig* (1843), the work of Bettina von Arnim, whose *Goethe's Briefwechsel mit einem Kind* had taken the literary world by storm in 1835. *Dies Buch,* which was begun in 1841 before Eugène Sue set the style, purported to be a series of dialogues with Frau Rat Goethe, which covered a variety of subjects, including civil liberties, capital punishment, and education as a safeguard against poverty and crime. The book caused considerable excitment; indeed, one government minister in 1844 considered it a direct cause of the weavers' uprising.[5] At the conclusion of Part II of the book (as an "Appendix to the Socratizing of Frau Rat"), there is a section entitled "The Experiences of a Young Swiss in Vogtland." Here, in a dry, sociological style, Bettina von Arnim recorded the observations of a student who had canvassed a slum district of Berlin which was then known as the "Vogtland" because of the large number of journeymen from Saxony who settled there. The neighborhood was razed later in the century to make room for the building of the Stettin Station. Giving streets and room numbers, she proceeded house by house to recount the terrible stories of unemployment and sickness which had brought the residents there. The following passages are typical.

In the opposite house (Gartenstrasse 92a), Room 9, lived journeyman carpenter Gellert. I did not find him at home. His mother-in-law lay deathly sick on some straw; his wife also seemed to be very sick; she stood erect with difficulty and told me that her husband had been without work for fourteen days and had now gone out to look for bread; the children were in school. The family had no outside help.

[5] K. A. Varnhagen von Ense, *Tagebuecher* (2d ed.; Leipzig and Hamburg, 1862–1905), II, 314. See also Ludwig Geiger, *Bettina von Arnim und Friedrich Wilhelm IV* (Frankfurt am Main, 1902), pp. 12–53.

In the same house, Room 72, I met Frau Schreyer. Her husband had been a poor man, a weaver who died in 1814, leaving her to bring up three children. The widow brought them up in the family house unsupported by anyone else. Only one son survives; he lives apart from his mother, and working as a weaver, barely makes a living for his own family. Frau Schreyer took up with another weaver for whom she makes bobbins, and so earns a few silver groschen. It should be noted that this woman must live with a man to whom she is not married in order to stave off hunger and unemployment. When he has no work, she too goes without food.

92b, Number 73. The weaver Fischer is forty-two years old. His appearance hardly inspires confidence; his disheveled hair, hollow eyes and ragged suit draw the attention of the police every time he goes into the street. At first glance it is clear that misery long ago cut off this man from decent society. . . . His wife looked like a sloven; her hair undone, she sat knitting on their dirty bed.[6]

No doubt the "Vogtland" of Berlin which Bettina von Arnim described had its counterpart in other German cities. But such cities, with their accumulations of human suffering, were few in number before 1850. Much more representative of social conditions than scenes from slum life were the village stories, or *Dorfgeschichten*, which began to appear in the 1840's.[7] The first writer to develop this genre in German literature was a Bernese clergyman, Albert Bitzius, who wrote under the pseudonym, "Jeremias Gotthelf." His *Bauernspiegel* (1837) and *Uli der Knecht* (1841), although moralizing in tone, were sternly realistic pictures of peasant life. The village story was picked up and developed in Germany proper by Berthold Auerbach, a

[6] Bettina von Arnim, *Saemtliche Werke* (Berlin, 1920–22), VI, 460, 462–63, 479–80.

[7] F. Altvater, *Wesen und Form der deutschen Dorfgeschichte* (Berlin, 1930); H. M. Waidson, *Jeremias Gotthelf* (Oxford, 1953); Berthold Auerbach, *Schrift und Volk, Grundzuege der volksthuemlichen Literatur* (Leipzig, 1846), pp. 386–406; Hanns Ernst Jansen, *Das Proletariat im Vormaerz in den Anschauungen deutscher Denker* (Kiel, 1928), pp. 60–66; M. I. Zwick, *Berthold Auerbachs sozialpolitischer und ethischer Liberalismus* (Stuttgart, 1933), pp. 59–88.

liberal, who, contrary to his own practice, warned his fellow writers to leave social and political problems to those who were trained to deal with them.

Auerbach's *Schwarzwaelder Dorfgeschichten* (1843) has no social message to preach; it is a collection of stories drawn from life and set in the Black Forest district of Wuerttemberg. Auerbach's peasants are not the rustic philosophers who appear in romantic poems or stories; neither are they brutes demoralized by hunger and privation. Most of them live frugally; indeed, they are so poor that idleness, sickness, or bad weather may bring severe hardship to entire families. But the general impression which Auerbach gives is not one of hardship. His peasants are occupied with hard work, simple pleasures, family sorrows, village rivalries and quarrels. Their lives follow a traditional routine which is only broken for some of them by military service or by emigration to America.

The peasants of the *Dorfgeschichten* are very like the peasants and the manual workers described by foreign travelers in Germany in the 1830's and 1840's. Observers from western Europe and the United States were impressed with the evidence that most of the people were poor but that few were in actual distress. Unused to peasant villages at home, Americans were shocked by the crowding and the dirt which they found in German villages. They were shocked also by the sight of women working in the fields and even on railroad gangs and by the general lack of material comforts. Noting their heavy, wadded clothing, an American essayist commented: "Poor Germans wear their fuel; all Germans wear their sidewalks in heavy boots; all wear their carpets in felt shoes; they are their own fences — cattle graze unfenced, but tended by women and children." [8]

----

[8] Nathaniel Parker Willis, "Invalid Rambles in Germany in 1845," *Rural Letters* (New York, 1853), pp. 278–79. See also Orville Dewey, *The Old World and the New* (New York, 1836), I, 175; Wilbur Fisk, *Travels in Europe* (5th ed.; New York, 1839), p. 447. Bayard Taylor's

William Howitt, an Englishman who lived for several years in Germany, was struck by the sight of peasants using cows as draft animals and often commented on the large numbers of people who lived, crowded together, in a single house. He observed that they had to work hard:

The women and children all work as well as the men, for it is family work; nay the women often work the hardest. They reap, thrash, mow, work on the fallows, do anything. . . . This would be thought a hard life in England; but hard as it is, it is not to be compared with the condition of labourers in some agricultural parts of a dear country like England, where eight or nine shillings a week, and no cow, no pig, nor fruit for the market, no work in the winter, but dependence for everything on a master, a constant feeling of anxiety, and the desperate prospect of ending his days in a Union workhouse, is too commonly the labourer's lot. The German peasants work hard, but they have no actual want.[9]

Howitt's observations on peasant life agree with those made at this time in other sectors of German society by the pioneer sociologist, Pierre LePlay. Conducting field studies of working-class conditions in several parts of Europe, LePlay wrote up case histories of a miner in the Harz Mountains and of a metalworker in Solingen. A life of hard work and thrift, he concluded, brought such workers in Germany just the minimum income they needed to provide the necessities of life and to save for their old age.[10]

While noting the general poverty in Germany, foreigners also remarked on the temperate habits of the working classes. Valentine Mott, a well-known New York surgeon attributed their sobriety to the fact that they were poor.

In travelling through Belgium, Holland, and Germany, particularly the latter extensive country, I was struck with the general

observations, made in 1844 and 1845, are in his *Views A-Foot* (rev. ed.; New York, 1862), pp. 152, 255.

[9] William Howitt, *The Rural and Domestic Life of Germany* (Philadelphia, 1843), p. 26.

[10] Pierre Le Play, *Les ouvriers européens* (2d ed.; Paris, 1877–79), III, 113–29, 158–64.

health and robustness of the population, attributable mainly to their frugal and regular habits of life, and to the general absence of all luxurious indulgences. The limited means of obtaining a livelihood compel every individual almost to a rigid economy and industry.[11]

A Scotsman who traveled widely in Europe and wrote on political economy, Samuel Laing, was amazed at the variety of public pleasures which the lower classes could enjoy; seeing their "eating houses, coffee-houses, dancing-rooms, concert-rooms, billiard-rooms, theatres, shows and balls," made him "sigh to think of our gin-palaces."[12] William Howitt in passage after passage contrasted the pleasant social life of the German workers with the drab existence of their counterparts in Britain. He attended open-air concerts in parks and palace gardens and noted: "The most striking thing to see is, how much is done everywhere for the public enjoyment of the people, and how perfectly natural they seem to think that it should be so." And again: "All are industrious, moderate in their desires, and disposed to enjoy themselves in a simple and unexpensive sociality; — music, books, the pleasures of summer sunshine and natural scenery are enjoyments amply offered and widely partaken."

Still another aspect of German society which deeply impressed foreigners was that it did not show the extremes of wealth and poverty which they saw in other countries. A typical reaction was that of an Englishman who, after traveling in Prussia and Saxony, asked rhetorically: "England may have reason to be proud of her sons when riches are talked of; what can she say when poverty is alluded to?

[11] Valentine Mott, *Travels in Europe and the East* (New York, 1842), p. 82. See also Jacques Matter, *De l'état moral, politique, et littéraire de l'Allemagne* (Paris, 1847), II, 216–18; Robert J. Breckenridge, *Memoranda of Foreign Travel* (Philadelphia, 1839), p. 98.

[12] Samuel Laing, *Observations on the Social and Political State of the European People in 1848 and 1849* (London, 1850), p. 463. See also Howitt, *Rural and Domestic Life*, pp. 110, 197.

Is it better . . . to have a thousand Croesuses, and millions who can scarcely gain a miserable pittance — than to have wealth generally diffused . . . ? The latter is actually the case here. . . ."[13] Jacques Matter, historian and moralist, saw signs of growing pauperism in the Wupper and Ruhr valleys but added that the rich looked after the welfare of the poor. T. C. Banfield had high praise for the paternalistic employers in the same area who provided their workers with "roomy, substantial" dwellings scattered in allotments which were usually cut out of former estates. Both Banfield and Laing admired the administration of poor relief and the public health service in Prussia.

A remark of Banfield's on conditions in northern Baden sums up very well the general impressions of travelers in many parts of Germany. He said that one would "observe with pleasure an absence of total destitution in any class of the inhabitants; but that a large portion of the population stands on the verge of great poverty, while a still greater number is involved in privations inseparable from the increase of mouths without a corresponding augmentation of the field of labour. . . ."[14] People standing on the verge of great poverty can be plunged into great suffering by such simple accidents as the loss of a market or a season of bad weather. An American who visited Frankfurt am Main in the summer of 1842 noted the robust, cheerful appearance of the people, and reported: "No careworn countenances, no sallow complexion, no premature old age — absolutely none." Bayard Taylor, who spent the long, rigorous winter of 1844–45 in Frankfurt, described how many of the poorer

[13] John Strang, *Germany in MDCCCXXXI* (London, 1836), II, 122–23; Fisk, *Travels*, p. 440; William Howitt, *German Experiences addressed to the English* (2d ed.; London, 1844), pp. 94, 100; Matter, *De l'état moral*, II, 230–31; Thomas Charles Banfield, *Industry of the Rhine, Series II: Manufactures* (London, 1848), pp. 45–46, 146–47; Samuel Laing, *Notes of a Traveller* (2d ed.; Philadelphia, 1846), pp. 239–52.

[14] Thomas Charles Banfield, *Industry of the Rhine, Series I: Agriculture* (London, 1846), p. 208. See also John Price Durbin, *Observations in Europe* (New York, 1844), I, 255–56; and Taylor, *Views A-Foot*, p. 152.

townspeople had been reduced to begging, and added: "It is painful to walk through the streets and see so many faces bearing plainly the marks of want, so many pale, hollow-eyed creatures, with suffering written on every feature." The condition of the Germans varied not only from year to year, as in Frankfurt, but from one part of the country to another. Certain districts, even whole provinces, suffered not only from occasional want but from persistent economic blight.

DISTRESSED AREAS

In some agrarian areas, there was permanent and wide-spread distress. In central and eastern Prussia a class of landless peasants had been developing partly as a result of land reforms, partly because of population increases.[15] Some of the members of this class who were attached to great estates as hired hands, or as *Instleute* (tenants who were allowed to occupy and work a small plot of land for themselves in return for their services on the estate proper), fared reasonably well. They were paid for their services both in money and in kind; they had steady work and a settled place to live. But the day laborers, or "free-workers," were badly off. Their work was irregular, and because their numbers grew faster than the demand for their services, their pay was low. Some of them migrated from one harvest to another, worked when they could on construction projects, such as railways and canals, and literally lived from hand to mouth. In western Germany the landless class was not as numerous, but in some areas, particularly on the west bank of the Rhine, the peasant proprietors owned plots which were too small or too unproductive to support them. Where they depended on the sale of a cash crop for their

---

[15] On the peasantry in eastern and central Prussia, see Erich Jordan, *Die Entstehung der konservativen Partei und die preussischen Agrarver-haeltnisse von 1848* (Munich, 1914), pp. 57–82; on conditions in the Rhineland and Westphalia, see Émile Jacquemin, *L'Allemagne agricole, industrielle et politique* (Paris, 1842), pp. 10–11, and Wilhelm Schulte, *Volk und Staat, Westfalen im Vormaerz und in der Revolution 1848–1849* (Muenster, 1954), pp. 111–23.

livelihood, as in the Moselle district, they competed against each other in a buyers' market with ruinous effects on their selling price. Even in the fertile province of Westphalia the land was too crowded to support all those who lived on it. For instance, in 1844, the area around Oerlinghausen had some 491 farms, of which only 81 were self-supporting. Over three-hundred landowners had to eke out their incomes by spinning and weaving.

The Rhineland and Westphalia were considered relatively prosperous elsewhere in Germany because the growth of new industries provided jobs and income for some of the surplus rural population.[16] But the dependence of the people on manufacturing for all or most of their livelihood had its drawbacks. For example, in Aachen, where the introduction of machinery seemed to threaten the security of the handworkers, there were repeated riots involving machine-smashing and incendiarism. Even industries which still made widespread use of the putting-out system gave rise to social problems, largely because they were extraordinarily susceptible to changes in the market. The silk industry around Krefeld, for example, lost much of its export trade in 1846 owing to a change in fashions. Some 3,000 looms out of 8,000 then fell idle; and 2,000 of the idle looms were those of domestic weavers who lived in the adjacent countryside. In Gladbach in the 1830's when the price of cotton yarn imported from England was increased by the levying of a tariff, the 6,500 looms producing cotton cloth for export were reduced to 1,500, and wages in the area fell off by 50 per cent. At the same time the linen industries centered in Muenster and Ravensberg in Westphalia were hard hit by the loss of their market to cotton manufacturers.

[16] On general conditions in the Rhineland, see Oscar J. Hammen, "Economic and Social Factors in the Prussian Rhineland in 1848," *American Historical Review*, LIV (1949), 825–40. For more detailed comments, see Alphons Thun, *Die Industrie am Niederrhein und ihre Arbeiter*; (ed.) Gustav Schmoller, *Staats -und sozialwissenschaftliche Forschungen*, II (1879), Heft I, 31–32, 112–13, 166–67; and Schulte, *Volk und Staat*, pp. 124–48.

By the late 1840's the latter city was sufficiently well known as a distressed area that when a group of workers in Louisville, Kentucky, collected $1,000 as a contribution to German relief they specified that $200 be distributed in Ravensberg.

The Erzgebirge and Vogtland districts of Saxony were areas which were widely known to be suffering from severe economic hardships.[17] They were mountainous districts, with poor soil and nearly exhausted ore deposits which had once supported a number of mining communities. To make a living, or to supplement the meagre living which the land afforded, miners and peasants turned to the spinning and weaving of cotton and the manufacture of stockings. When the market for these products fell off, the people went hungry.

The most notorious of the distressed areas in Germany was, of course, Silesia. Because both contemporary observers and subsequent historians have drawn false generalizations from Silesian conditions, they deserve our close attention. Much of the land in that province was unproductive, and so, for generations, Silesian families had supported themselves by "domestic" industries, principally the raising and spinning of flax and the weaving of linen.[18] The paternalistic Habsburgs had given the Silesian linen industry special protection, and Frederick the Great continued their policies after his seizure of the province. Silesian linen was of relatively high quality and was relatively cheap; it had extensive sales in foreign markets and brought a steady flow of money into the province. The results of this pros-

[17] Otto Hué, *Die Bergarbeiter* (Stuttgart, 1913), II, 125–29; Mathilde Klemm, *Sachsen und die deutsche Problem, 1848* (Meissen, 1914), pp. 5–6; Hedwig Maass, *Von Frauenarbeit zu Frauenfabrikarbeit* (Heidelberg, 1938), pp. 66–67.

[18] Zimmermann, *Bluethe und Verfall*, pp. 12–25, 73–84, 281–337; Wilhelm Wolff, "Das Elend und der Aufruhr in Schlesien," *Gesammelte Schriften* (Berlin, 1909), pp. 44–46; Gertrud Hermes, "Statistische Studien zum zollvereinten Deutschland," *Archiv fuer Sozialwissenschaft und Sozialpolitik,* LXIII (1930), 139–40. On the condition of Silesian miners, see Hué, *Bergarbeiter*, II, 24–25.

perity were population growth, local specialization in linen manufacturing, and continued increase in the numbers of those engaged in the industry.

Early in the nineteenth century, the industry fell on hard times. Everywhere linen lost out to cotton cloth, and whatever market remained was captured by Irish or Belgian hand-loomed material or by cheap, machine-made English material. Even within the Zollverein tariffs were too low to protect the Silesians from foreign competition. Many of them turned to the spinning and weaving of cotton, but they could not begin to compete with more efficient producers in western Europe. Either too poor or too unimaginative to emigrate, mechanize, or turn to some other line of production, they tried to meet competing prices by cheapening the quality of their cloth, a desperate measure which only cut further into their market. The decline of the textile trade hurt not only those immediately engaged in it but also depressed the economy of the entire province. Silesian miners, for instance, were known to be the worst paid and the worst treated in Germany.

In the summer of 1840, Frederick William IV visited Silesia, saw the poverty of his subjects, and ordered his ministers to take some remedial steps. A large plant for the preparing and spinning of linen was to be set up by the government at Erdmannsdorf; and Prussian consuls were to explore all possibilities of reopening foreign markets for Silesian linen. But nothing the government did served to ease the distress. In 1842 a bad local potato crop deprived many families of their chief source of nourishment and led directly to some cases of death by starvation and to an outbreak of "hunger typhus." Some unscrupulous employers — in particular, the middlemen who bought cloth from the weavers — took advantage of their distress by driving down the prices they would pay. The daily wage for common, unskilled labor in Silesia at that time was approximately ten silver groschen, a wage generally considered to be the rock-bottom minimum necessary to support a family of four. For a length of cloth which required nine days to weave, the more humane firms paid the weaver thirty-two silver groschen, while others, like Zwanziger Brothers in Peterswaldau, paid only fifteen silver groschen.[19] Meanwhile humanitarians and writers eager to capitalize on the public's newly stimulated taste for stories of poverty and despair turned out heart-rending accounts of the weavers' condition. Relief committees were organized in the county seats of the province as well as in the capital, Breslau, and by February, 1844, even in Berlin and the Rhineland.

Late in March, 1844, the Ministry of the Interior in Berlin sent a worried note to the chief administrative officer in Silesia, *Oberpraesident* Friedrich Theodor von Merckel, asking him whether or not the weavers needed some form of state aid.[20] Merckel, the son of a Breslau linen merchant, had been educated at the University of Halle in the heyday of Adam Smith's influence there. As an official in the Prussian government, he had been closely associated with Stein, Schoen, and other reformers in the period after 1806. He became *Oberpraesident* of Silesia in 1816 and, except for a few years between 1820 and 1825, occupied the post until 1845. To Berlin's request for advice in the spring of 1844, Merckel answered early in April that no state aid would be necessary. He minimized the extent of the weavers' hardships and said that journalists and special pleaders like Friedrich List had written exaggerated reports to strengthen their arguments on behalf of higher tariff protection for the Zollverein's textile producers. He acknowledged that the weavers were hard hit but pointed out that they had been poor before and that they would simply have to wait for an upturn in the trade cycle. There was no immediate

[19] Wolff, "Das Elend," p. 50; Zimmermann, *Bluethe und Verfall*, pp. 337–43; Alexander Schneer, *Ueber die Noth der Leinen-Arbeiter in Schlesien* (Berlin, 1844), pp. 69–72.

[20] Zimmermann, *Bluethe und Verfall*, pp. 343–46. On Merckel, see *Allgemeine deutsche Biographie*, XXI, 406–7; on Merckel's early career, see Otto Lincke, *Friedrich Theodor von Merckel im Dienste fuers Vaterland* (Berlin, 1907–10).

danger of mass starvation; meanwhile railroad and highway construction work would provide all the relief the
weavers needed.

On June 3, 1844, the weavers of Peterswaldau in *Kreis*
Reichenbach gathered outside the Zwanzigers' house and
demonstrated for higher pay.[21] Zwanziger had one of the
demonstrators arrested. The next day rioting broke out
which lasted over a period of thirty-six hours and resulted
in the gutting of Zwanzigers' property but left that of the
more generous employers untouched. The rioters then
marched to the neighboring town of Langenbielau and
there plundered two more establishments. A third came
under attack but was saved by a small detachment of infantry. In the scuffle between troops and rioters, eleven of
the latter were shot dead, and twenty-four were wounded.
On the morning of June 6, Merckel arrived in *Kreis* Reichenbach along with three companies of infantry, some artil-
lery pieces, and a squad of cavalry. Roughly one hundred
participants in the riot were arrested, eighty of whom were
sentenced to prison. Once quiet was restored, Merckel
recommended to Berlin that the government encourage
employers to treat the weavers more favorably. Failing that,
he urged a broader program of public works to give them
jobs, a course of action which did, in fact, prove to be
the more effective immediate means of relief.

A minor incident in itself, the uprising of the Silesian
weavers came to occupy a place in the German public consciousness comparable to that of the "Peterloo" massacre
of 1819 in the mind of the English public. The subject was
taken up not only by poets and novelists but by dramatists
and painters as well. A large canvas depicting the oppression of the weavers was exhibited in Cologne in July, 1844.
From there it went on tour and everywhere on its tour attracted sizeable crowds. It was also widely circulated in

[21] Zimmermann, *Bluethe und Verfall*, pp. 350–79; Liptzin, *The Weavers*,
pp. 19–26; Karl Biedermann, *Dreissig Jahre deutscher Geschichte, 1840–
1870* (2d ed.; Breslau, 1883), I, 157–58.

lithographed reproductions. An excited debate went on in the press about the actual causes of the weavers' distress and about the government's conduct in the matter. With perfect justice, Friedrich Harkort, a Westphalian industrialist with philanthropic interests, remarked in 1845: "The great question of the times — improving the lot of the lower classes — has recently, since the events in Silesia which speak louder than prophetic voices, made its inevitable entry into the foreground of the religious and political scene." [22] Certainly, conditions in Silesia were exceptional, but much of the excitement about events there in 1844 was caused by a widespread sense that they were a forecast of things to come within the predictable future to other parts of Germany. The weavers' uprising focused attention on social problems generally and, by coincidence, did so just before all of Europe slid into a brief but grievous period of general economic depression.

ECONOMIC CYCLES

Germany suffered from the general economic paralysis which gripped post-Napoleonic Europe well into the 1820's. Because of the diminished buying power of consumers, grain prices and land values fell off by as much as 50 per cent. [23] A few crop failures in the 1820's and the raising of tariff barriers in Britain and France made the depression particularly severe in those areas which depended for their income on exporting food to foreign markets. By 1830,

[22] Friedrich Harkort, *Die Vereine zur Hebung der untern Volksclassen* (Elberfeld, 1845), p. 20.

[23] A. Ucke, *Die Agrarkrisis in Preussen waehrend der zwanziger Jahre dieses Jahrhunderts* (Halle, 1888), pp. 14–20. The best general account is in Siegfried von Ciriacy-Wantrup, *Agrarkrisen und Stockungsspannen* (Berlin, 1936), pp. 2–102. Price fluctuations are graphed in B. Foeldes, "Die Getreidepreise im neunzehnten Jahrhundert," *Jahrbuecher fuer Nationaloekonomie und Statistik*, Ser. III, XXIX (1905), 483. On southwestern Germany, see Sigmund Fleischmann, *Die Agrarkrise von 1844–1845 mit besonderer Beruecksichtigung von Baden* (Heidelberg, 1902); and Paul Gehring, "Das Wirtschaftsleben unter Koenig Wilhelm I," *Zeitschrift fuer wuerttembergische Landesgeschichte*, IX (1949), 196–256.

however, agricultural Germany began to enjoy a gradual recovery. Gross production increased thanks to improved methods of cultivation. Grain prices went up; in Prussia, for instance, the price of wheat and rye rose by an average of 40 per cent to 45 per cent in the twenty years between 1829 and 1849. At the same time, the cost of labor remained constant, or nearly so, and allowed a sharp rise in net profits. A reliable index of agricultural prosperity in the 1830's was the recovery of land values and the decline in the number of foreclosures on mortgaged land. The owners of the large farms and estates in northern and eastern Germany profited most from the rise in farm prices, but the small farmers of the southern and western parts of the country profited too, especially where more intensive farming had begun to increase the yield on their holdings. Weather conditions remained favorable throughout the decade, with the result that between 1830 and 1842 there was no major crop failure.

The economic recovery of the 1830's was interrupted in the mid-1840's by a series of bad harvests. Difficulties began in the summer of 1842 with a drought that parched most of Germany well into the autumn. Crop losses were heavy but not calamitous in themselves. Reserves, however, began to dwindle in 1842 and continued to do so in 1843 and 1845, both years of subaverage yields. Food shortages in Germany became acute in 1845 with the coming of a potato blight which destroyed nearly half of the harvest. Germans generally were not as dependent as the Irish on potatoes for their food, but, according to one Pomeranian agriculturalist, potatoes did make up four-fifths of the diet of the poor in some areas.[24] The crisis grew more acute in 1846 when once again blight rotted potatoes in fields and storage cellars. The rye crop was also very bad, and the

---

[24] Ernst von Buelow-Cummerow, *Preussen im Januar 1847 und das Patent von 3 Februar* (Berlin, 1847), pp. 27–30; Paul Roemisch, *Ueber Kornteuerung und deren moegliche Verhuetung* (Frankfurt am Main, 1855), *passim*.

yields of other grains and vegetables were down by some 25 per cent from their averages; losses raised the spectre of famine in those communities which, even in good years, lived on the margin of subsistence.

Governments of several German states took immediate steps to meet the crisis; with the exception of Prussia, they banned the export of food and removed duties on food imports. They bought some food in central Europe, where it was available, and imported grain from Russia and the United States for distribution to communities which had used up their reserves. Partly because of government purchasing, partly because of hoarding by bakers and merchants, and partly because of private speculation in grain futures, food prices shot up and many farmers who had food to sell withheld it from the market in anticipation of higher prices.[25] Food prices reached their peak in the spring of 1847 and brought such hardship to town dwellers that food riots broke out in towns from the Baltic to the Danube; Stettin, Eisleben, Frankfurt am Oder, Merseburg, Halle, Nuernberg, Wittenberg, Dresden, and Ulm became scenes of angry and disorderly demonstrations against high prices. In April, the "potato revolution" was touched off in Berlin when a mob of infuriated shoppers roughed up a farm wife in the public market. Rioting spread through the city, shop windows were broken, "profiteers" were manhandled, and, at the height of the disorders, one of the royal palaces was attacked. Quiet was restored the next day, and some observers hinted darkly that the mob had been aroused by adventurous liberals in the United Diet which had just opened its sessions in Berlin. But, according to testimony taken in court from arrested rioters, the mob was made up of hungry, angry people and had no political direction

---

[25] Hanns Leiskow, *Spekulation und oeffentliche Meinung in der ersten Haelfte des neunzehnten Jahrhunderts* (Jena, 1930), pp. 65–70; Fleischmann, *Agrarkrise*, pp. 9–51; Dora Meyer, *Das oeffentliche Leben in Berlin im Jahr vor der Maerzrevolution* (Berlin, 1912), pp. 81–98; Karl Biedermann, *Geschichte des ersten preussischen Reichstags* (Leipzig, 1847), pp. 130–31.

whatever. Better harvests in 1847 brought some falloff in food prices, although crops were not good enough to dispel all the anxiety which had arisen in the previous year.

The agricultural crisis of the mid-1840's coincided with, and intensified, a trade crisis which began as the result of a money shortage. This, in turn, resulted in large part from overinvestment in railways.[26] In November, 1842, the Prussian government, desiring to divert capital from government securities into more productive investments, guaranteed investors a return of 3.5 per cent on railway stocks. During the next eighteen months, stock exchanges in Berlin, Frankfurt am Main, and Breslau were scenes of frenzied trading as railway companies were formed overnight and their stock issues were wildly oversubscribed. In 1843, for example, the Saxon-Silesian Railway Company called for six million thalers and got fifty-six million. The Cologne-Krefeld line called for two and one-quarter million and got fifty-three million. In May, 1844, the Ministry of Finance decided to cut off speculation in railways by announcing a series of controls on investors and brokers. A mild panic followed in which shares fell off by 10 per cent to 20 per cent. Although railway building continued in the late 1840's, many companies were hobbled by the difficulty of getting new capital. Meanwhile large sums of money had been sunk into developing a transportation network which could only pay for itself over a period of many years.

An atmosphere of gloom settled on German business in the later 1840's which can be explained only in part by economic causes.[27] Investment capital was hard to get; discount rates rose; Germany began to feel, although still only slightly, the shock waves of international crises like those

[26] Leiskow, *Spekulation*, pp. 9–37; Joseph Hansen, *Gustav von Mevissen, ein rheinisches Lebensbild, 1815–1894* (Berlin, 1906), I, 427–28.

[27] Max Wirth, *Geschichte der Handelskrisen* (4th ed.; Frankfurt am Main, 1890), p. 241; Wilhelm Roepke, *Crises and Cycles* (London, 1936), p. 41; Arthur Spiethoff, "Krisen," *Handwoerterbuch der Staatswissenschaften*, ed. Ludwig Elster and Johannes Conrad (4th ed.; Jena, 1923–28), VI, 8–91.

of 1847 which, beginning in London, spread to commercial houses in Paris, Amsterdam, Bremen, Hamburg, and St. Petersburg. These spasms, when they affected western Europe and the United States in the 1830's, left Germany virtually untouched. Such spasms usually followed surges of optimism which led to overinvestment which, in turn, brought on shortages of money — at bottom, shortages of gold. The fact that the German economy began in the 1840's to feel the effects of events in London was a sign of economic growth. Still German business in this period seemed to suffer less from a shortage of money than from a loss of public confidence. Rumblings of social discontent in France and England together with the Silesian uprising raised some second thoughts about the desirability of industrial development and some fears for the security of property. The growing political unrest in Europe made the whole future dark and uncertain.

The tremulous state of public confidence in the later 1840's shows up very clearly in the story of the failure and recovery in 1847 of the banking firm of S. von Haber and Sons of Frankfurt am Main.[28] The House of Haber, which had a branch in Karlsruhe, had invested heavily in three of the chief industries of Baden, a spinning mill in Ettlingen, a machine shop in Karlsruhe, and a beet sugar refinery in Waghaeusel. The firm had, in fact, overcommitted itself, and unable to attract the money it needed to make good its obligations, it began a monthly or weekly game of bill-jobbing. Local demands were met with a draft on a bank in Strasbourg, which was covered with a draft on a bank in Augsburg, which, in turn, was covered by a draft on a bank in Frankfurt, and so on. Some banking houses saw through the game, among them the House of Rothschild, which one day refused to honor Habers' draft. A run on the House of Haber followed, and the bank was forced to stop payments. In Baden where

[28] Wirth, *Geschichte*, pp. 242–44.

the failure of the Habers threatened to close down three factories, the fate of the bank became a public issue. A business group in Mannheim wanted the three factories put into receivership; the government, however, decided to intervene. Creditors of the bank were asked to let their investments stand, and in return the government guaranteed the payment of interest and the amortization of their debts within fifteen years. This action of the government was sufficient to restore confidence. The House of Haber got the money it needed; the bank and the industries were saved; and the government did not have to make good its guarantees.

Actually, the depression of the late 1840's was quite superficial and might have been short-lived. The coincidence of a trade crisis with an agricultural crisis made it seem worse than it was; the revolutionary outbreaks of 1848 prolonged it for several years. But a few bountiful harvests were enough to restore prosperity to German agriculture; the gold strikes in California (1848) and Australia (1851) were enough to ease the international money shortage. Meanwhile the slow buildup of productive capacity in the 1830's and 1840's began, after 1850, to make consumer goods more abundant and less expensive than they had been. Germany in the 1830's had, in fact, entered on a period of gradual economic improvement which lasted until the end of the century.[29] This long wave of rising prosperity was broken at several points in its career by short downturns, such as the one following 1844. The first dip in the rising curve brought hunger and anxiety to thousands of Germans and was the direct occasion for an outburst of articles and pamphlets which expressed a well-founded concern about the spread of pauperism. The fact that Dieterici, the statistician, could at the same time answer these pessimists by pointing to economic gains al-

[29] Joseph A. Schumpeter, *Business Cycles* (New York, 1939), II, 351; Hermes, "Statistische Studien," p. 123; Spiethoff, "Krisen," p. 50.

ready made and forecasting, correctly, greater gains to come was a paradox but not a contradiction.

<h2 style="text-align:center">STATISTICAL ANALYSES</h2>

The art of gathering statistics matured rather slowly in early nineteenth-century Germany.[30] Too often the statistical offices then established by the governments were dependent for their data on untrained, overworked clerks and officials in other agencies; seldom did they make any sustained effort at guaranteeing uniformity. J. G. Hoffmann, head of the Prussian Statistical Bureau from 1806 to 1844, refused even to try to collect figures on such difficult subjects as the causes of death or certain aspects of agricultural production. Gaps were left in official compilations which later historians could fill only by interpolation or enlightened conjecture. Approximate and incomplete as they are, the available statistics on the production and consumption of goods and on the movement of wages and prices in Germany during the 1830's and 1840's help us to refine our notion of social conditions and to understand the dimensions of the social problem.

Wilhelm Dieterici's statistical study of conditions in Prussia in the early nineteenth century traces an almost unbroken march of progress from 1806 to the early 1840's.[31] His figures on capital development and increases in gross production are impressive, but more interesting are his estimates of increases in consumption. According to these, the per capita consumption of wheat in Prussia increased by 20 per cent between 1831 and 1842, while consumption of rye fell off slightly, a shift usually indicative of good times in Germany. Per capita consumption of meat increased 11 per cent in the same period; that of sugar, 25 per cent; that of coffee, 10 per cent. But levels of consump-

---

[30] For comments on the accuracy of statistics at this time, see Wilhelm Dieterici, *Der Volkswohlstand im preussischen Staate* (Berlin, 1846), p. 251; August Meitzen, *Geschichte, Theorie, und Technik der Statistik* (Berlin, 1886), *passim*.

[31] Dieterici, *Volkswohlstand*, esp. pp. 131–35, 197–208.

tion remained relatively low. Dieterici estimated that the average Prussian by 1842 was buying annually the following amounts of food and soft goods: six bushels of grain, thirty-five pounds of meat, thirteen quarts of beer, six quarts of brandy, two quarts of wine, three-quarters of a pound of rice, five pounds of sugar, two and one-half pounds of coffee, a small quantity of spices, seventeen pounds of salt, three pounds of tobacco, about one yard of wool, three yards of linen, somewhat over nine yards of cotton, less than a yard of silk, and a small quantity of leather. For these he would have had to pay nearly twenty-four thalers in 1806; in 1842 he paid just above twenty-two thalers. Greater abundance and lower prices of consumer goods were, unfortunately, not complemented by lower housing costs. While construction of public buildings, factories, mills, warehouses, and, most notably, farm buildings shot ahead, that of private housing did not keep pace with population growth. The inevitable results were high rents and high purchase prices on dwelling units.

Dieterici's cheerful calculations did not, of course, go unchallenged; his sources and his methods were subjected to severe criticism.[32] His figures, drawn from reports to government officials, were considered particularly unreliable for the decade 1806 to 1816, a period when farmers found it easy to lie about their harvests and livestock in order to cheat the tax collector, and when a lively trade was conducted through illegal channels. The quantities of foodstuffs bought and sold on the black market did not show up in government reports. Dieterici could justly boast of great increases in national wealth; but what about the inequities in the distribution of that wealth? For example, he could quite correctly point out that since the acreage of land under cultivation had increased, agricultural production had increased; but he glossed over the fact that these increases were made in large part by di-

[32] W. Lueders, "Der Volkswohlstand im preussischen Staate," *Die Epigonen*, IV (1847), 252–95.

viding common lands and depriving the very poor of the main source of their livelihood. Or again, per capita figures on consumption can be a very misleading index of the standard of life among the poor.

How general was the prosperity of 1830 to 1845 in Germany? From a thorough study of the statistical data of Dieterici and other compilers, it seems clear that most Germans benefited, but in varying degrees.[33] Obviously, the proprietors of small and medium-sized farms did not profit to the same extent as did the proprietors of large farms and estates who sold their produce in a highly favorable export market. The fact that the estate owners, particularly those in central and eastern Prussia, were growing wealthier at this time is of prime importance for understanding their ability to ride out the storms of 1848 and 1849 and to consolidate their power before the new industrial class was strong enough to challenge them. The fortunes of the commercial and industrial classes were certainly rising in the 1830's and 1840's, but their enterprises were as yet too new and too small to pay very large returns. Meanwhile, some members of the artisan class suffered from the competition of the new industries, but a great many others enjoyed the general prosperity until the mid-1840's.

The small but growing class of factory workers in Germany between 1800 and 1850 has been the subject of a recent and extensive study by the Marxist historian, Juergen Kuczynski.[34] His main thesis is that in the early or "primitive" period of industrial capitalism, "competition on the foreign market and the relative technical stagnation in German factories made the German employer rely more and more for a secure flow of profits on the brutal exploitation of his workers." Brushing aside Dieterici's figures on per capita consumption, Kuczynski makes his point

[33] Hermes, "Statistische Studien," pp. 130–41.
[34] Juergen Kuczynski, *A Short History of Labour Conditions under Capitalism* (London, 1942–45), III, 11–63.

by citing evidence drawn almost exclusively from the most distressed areas of Germany in the most depressed years. In his text and bibliography he refers to some fifty pamphlets which expressed alarm at the spread of pauperism. All but two of these pamphlets appeared between the years 1845 and 1850. He refers repeatedly to reports on Silesia by Wilhelm Wolff and Alexander Schneer, as though Silesian conditions were representative of the entire country. In the face of statistics which show that the consumption of beer and spirits was declining during this period and in contradiction to other evidence of the sobriety of the German poor, he supports his claim that alcoholism was a growing problem by a reference to "Briefe aus dem Wuppertal," one of Friedrich Engels' juvenilia.

Kuczynski's evidence is lopsided but not entirely false. Unquestionably, some German industrialists mistreated their workers. Short of money to meet payrolls, they fell back on the truck system; and because of a surplus supply of manpower, they could exact long hours for low wages.[35] Kuczynski's estimates of gross wages, admittedly sketchy, do not vary markedly from the estimates of other authorities. Day laborers in farming areas were the worst paid group in the country. Their wages showed very little change from 1820 to the late 1840's, a fact which, when taken together with rises in living costs, meant that their real income was declining. By contrast, the industrial wage earners fared much better. Between 1820 and 1847, wages in the textile industries rose by averages of from 42.8 to 63.3 per cent; wages in mining and the heavy industries rose by averages of from 94 to 100 per cent.[36]

Computing real wages, that is, wages in terms of purchasing power, is difficult because rising and falling food

[35] Guenther Anton, *Geschichte der preussischen Fabrikgesetzgebung*; Gustav Schmoller (ed.), *Staats- und sozialwissenschaeftliche Forschungen*, XI (1891), Heft I, 1–82, 133–202.

[36] Arnold Frege, *Zur Lohnbewegung der letzten hundert Jahre* (Leipzig, n.d. [*ca.* 1865]), p. 29; Pierre Benaerts, *Les origines de la grande industrie allemande* (Paris, 1933), p. 581.

prices brought pronounced year-to-year fluctuations in living costs. Table 2 shows Kuczynski's estimates. The general rising trend evident in the figures in Table 2 was bound to hurt the rural day laborers whose wages had leveled off during this period. The only mitigating circumstance was that many of them, living on the soil, had sources of food other than the retail grocers. Industrial workers, on the other hand, appear between 1820 and 1847 to have earned wages which kept pace reasonably well with rises in the cost of living, except in the bad years 1846 and 1847.

TABLE 2
Cost of Living
(1900 = 100)

Year	Index	Year	Index	Year	Index
1820	49	1830	50	1840	53
1821	43	1831	57	1841	52
1822	44	1832	54	1842	55
1823	45	1833	52	1843	58
1824	36	1834	45	1844	53
1825	35	1835	46	1845	57
1826	39	1836	45	1846	68
1827	46	1837	46	1847	79
1828	47	1838	52	1848	57
1829	48	1839	54	1849	50

* Juergen Kuczynski, *A Short History of Labour Conditions under Capitalism* London, 1942–45), III, 32.

According to a recent estimate, at least 50 to 60 per cent of the German population in this period did not have a secure livelihood.[37] These were the millions who, even with good luck and in good times, lived, as Banfield put it, "on the verge of great poverty." Undeniably, the economic advances which the country had made in the 1830's and early 1840's held promise of deliverance; but the hardships which many Germans suffered in the late 1840's were more acute and more widespread than any in memory. From this mixed scene of progress and suffering different observers drew different conclusions. Many liberals concerned with social problems agreed with their socialist and conservative critics that liberal social reforms had gone

[37] Werner Conze, "Vom 'Poebel' zum 'Proletariat,' sozialgeschichtliche Voraussetzungen fuer den Sozialismus in Deutschland," *Vierteljahrschrift fuer Sozial- und Wirtschaftsgeschichte*, XLI (1954), 333–64.

too far toward atomizing society and removing traditional safeguards against pauperism. They agreed that the cure for social ills should be sought in a return to some measure of state and corporate regulation of the economy. But for other liberals who were less concerned with immediate problems, the only hope for the future was continued economic growth and such growth would continue only so long as businessmen were free to take risks and to collect high rewards if successful. The remedy for the distress of the 1840's was, in their opinion, not more, but less, regulation.

III

The Argument for Free Enterprise

None of the liberals who wrote on social questions were deductive thinkers reasoning from first principles to specific recommendations for economic and social policies. Rather, they worked from observations of particular circumstances to general statements of policy, and the value of their contributions to social thought depended very much on the range and acuteness of their observations. Since most of the liberals who argued for free enterprise were men of affairs who were themselves caught up in the economic revolution, their ideas frequently seem to grow out of shallow, chance impressions rather than any systematic body of observations. But frequently, too, their activities produced insights into the workings of society which escaped the more speculative thinkers.

KARL HEINRICH RAU

One of the most persuasive advocates of free enterprise in the 1830's and 1840's was the academician and public servant, Karl Heinrich Rau (1792–1870).[1] Born and educated at Erlangen, a Protestant community in Bavaria, where his father was a pastor and professor of theology at the university, Rau completed his university studies in 1812 and two years later began to teach at the local secondary school. In 1817 he was commissioned by the Ba-

---

[1] On Rau's career, see Friedrich Weech, *Badische Biographien* (Heidelberg, 1875–81), II, 147–60; *Allgemeine deutsche Biographie*, XXVII, 380–85. On his views, see Karl Neumann, *Die Lehren K. H. Raus* (Giessen, 1927).

varian government to travel, observe, and report on the organization of agriculture and the use of new farming methods in northern and central Germany. The next year he was appointed to a professorship at the University of Giessen, and in 1822 he accepted a call from the university of Heidelberg where he remained as a professor of political economy for the rest of his active life.

Rau's importance as a teacher was considerable; he shaped the outlook of most government officials of Baden for nearly half a century. His interest and competence in practical affairs repeatedly brought him out of the lecture hall into administrative work at Heidelberg and advisory work for the government of Baden, and these experiences influenced his thinking on political economy quite as much as his reading. For many years he was the university's chief adviser on financial questions. He was first named a court councilor in 1822, then a privy councilor in 1845 for his services to the government in Karlsruhe. In 1833, 1835, and 1837, he represented the University of Heidelberg in the Diet of Baden where he voted with the moderate liberals and worked on committees which studied such questions as railway construction and the abolition of tithes. After 1848, when he was a member of the Frankfurt *Vorparlament*, Rau's political activities tapered off somewhat, and so did his scholarly production. By that date he had been converted to the principles of free enterprise, and nothing in later life caused him to change his mind.

Strangely enough Rau began his career as a spirited opponent of liberal reforms. In 1816 and 1820, he published two prize-winning essays, one criticizing the dissolution of the guilds, the other denouncing such modern innovations as the division of labor and the use of labor-saving machinery. In his *Ansichten der Volkswirtschaft*, the fruit of his year's travel and study for the Bavarian government, he stressed the need for taking local conditions into account in formulating economic and social policies and, in effect, repudiated the notion that these policies should rest only on universally valid, natural laws.[2] Meanwhile he raised detailed objections to free enterprise in his translation and commentary on the works of a Russian disciple of Adam Smith, Heinrich Friedrich von Storch.[3] Storch's *Cours d'économie politique* was an effort to apply Adam Smith's doctrine to the Russian economy, an effort which forced Storch to modify a good many of his master's theories. Rau, in his commentary, went well beyond Storch in criticism of Adam Smith, particularly in opposing an organic theory of the state to the negative, mechanical view, he found in *The Wealth of Nations.*

Rau's gradual conversion to free enterprise began in the 1820's; there is evidence of this change in his *Lehrbuch der politischen Oekonomie*, a manual published several years after his call to Heidelberg. Solid and rather pedestrian, the *Lehrbuch* was Rau's most important work and remained for a generation the standard textbook in its field; it went through numerous reprintings and revisions and, translated into eight languages, gave its author an international reputation. The progress of his conversion can be followed in the pages of the *Archiv der politischen Oekonomie und Polizeiwissenschaft*, a quarterly review, which Rau founded in 1835 and continued to publish until 1852 when it was merged with the *Zeitschrift fuer die gesammte Staatswissenschaft*.[4] The extent of his conversion can be measured in a university address, delivered at Heidelberg in November, 1847, and published under the title,

[2] Rau's early works were *Ueber das Zunftwesen und die Folgen seiner Aufhebung* (Leipzig, 1816); *Ueber die Ursachen der Armuth* ("Von der Harlemer Gesellschaft gekroente Preisschrift" [1820]); *Ansichten der Volkswirtschaft* (Leipzig, 1821).

[3] H. F. von Storch, *Cours d'économie politique* (St. Petersburg, 1815); Rau's translation appeared as *Handbuch der Nationalwirtschaftslehre* (Hamburg, 1817–19).

[4] See in particular Rau's review of Friedrich List's *Das nationale System der politischen Oekonomie*, in *Archiv der politischen Oekonomie*, V (1843), 252–97, 349–412.

Ueber die Beschraenkungen der Freiheit in der Volkswirt-schaftpflege.

While he wrote no articles or treatises dealing specifically with the social problem, Rau, in his *Lehrbuch* and elsewhere, did take up the subject of poverty, its causes and how it may be counteracted.[5] He reaffirmed the liberals' belief in economic and social progress not as inevitable but as possible, and he rejected the pessimistic view that mass poverty is the unavoidable result of the tendency of men to breed faster than they can increase their food supply. In advanced civilizations, he argued, men can and do exercise some control over their numbers; and, what is more important, they can vastly increase their production of the necessities of life. He pointed out that a rise in the number of available workers need not cause a drop in wages so long as capital is present to create new enterprises and so to provide jobs for more workers. In fact, population growth, if accompanied by an increase in capital, will force the pace of economic progress. Poverty, where it arises, is the result of a fortuitous and temporary maladjustment between capital and population, or stated more broadly, between supply and demand. Such maladjustments are usually caused by chance events, by too bountiful or too meagre harvests, by exaggerated speculation leading to loss of confidence, or by fluctuations in the market owing to war or the threat of war. Economic growth, according to Rau, was normal rather than automatic; poverty and social dislocation were accidents. Accidents would unfortunately happen, and so he cautioned men to prepare for them.

According to Rau, men could take collective action to protect themselves against adversity either through voluntary associations or through the state.[6] By the time he

[5] Karl Heinrich Rau, *Lehrbuch der politischen Oekonomie* (Heidelberg, 1826–28), II, 12–15, 147–48, 378–79; Neumann, *Lehren*, p. 96.

[6] Rau, *Lehrbuch*, II, 44–147, 199–201, 332–40; Neumann, *Lehren*, pp. 76–96.

published his manual of political economy he had come to endorse *Gewerbefreiheit*, but he admitted that guild regulations could still on occasion be useful. For example, a limit to be determined annually on the number of artisans permitted to ply any particular trade in any particular area would prevent overcrowding of that trade. He approved of workers' associations for educational purposes and for the relief of members in times of distress. He also favored both producers' and consumers' co-operatives. As for the state, it had a threefold responsibility for the welfare of its citizens. First, it should educate all classes, rural and urban, through trade schools, agricultural schools, model farms, and nurseries, so that every worker would have an opportunity to develop his skill to the maximum. Further, the state should sponsor working-class associations by encouraging, but not forcing, employers to recognize and help those associations. Finally, the state must intervene directly to regulate the economy when the free play of economic laws would bring distress to some group or class. Free trade, for instance, is generally desirable, but customs barriers must never be lowered to a point where large numbers of people would be deprived of a living. Free competition should not be confused with license to behave irresponsibly or dishonestly. The state must take action to prevent adulteration of food and to enforce the observance of safety precautions in places of work. Rau did not go so far, however, as to advocate the prohibition of child labor.

In extreme cases, then, Rau conceded that the state had a duty to intervene in the economic affairs of its citizens.[7] But with increasing frequency and emphasis he urged that such acts of intervention be regarded as exceptional and undertaken only after mature study and consideration.

[7] K. H. Rau, "Ueber den Nutzen, den gegenwaertigen Zustand, und die neueste Literatur der Nationaloekonomie," *Archiv der politischen Oekonomie*, I (1835), 11–12.

Otherwise, he feared, the state would be seduced into legislating in behalf of particular interest groups to the detriment of the majority. He noted that the state was subjected to the most contradictory demands: to guarantee food supplies, conduct relief agencies, forestall trade crises, give free rein to businessmen, and reduce the taxes of businessmen. These demands came from selfish groups that wanted the best of both worlds. They wanted both maximum security and freedom of operation for themselves and cared neither how their security impinged upon the freedom of others nor how their freedom destroyed the security of others. So long as their special interests were served they did not worry about the principle of equality before the law.

Government intervention was dangerous, in Rau's opinion, not only because it would lead to inequities but also because it could never be a sovereign remedy for all economic ailments. The state was not omnicompetent; even with the best intentions and the most extensive controls, it could not ensure the well-being of all of its citizens. One man's gain might be another man's misfortune; long-range advances were often made at the expense of short-term losses. Should the state rush to the aid of the disadvantaged at every turn in fortune's wheel? Should the state, for example, ban the use of machinery to save the artisans from technological unemployment? The end result might be economic damage far greater in scope and more permanent than the original harm done to the artisans. The most successful government measures, Rau believed, were those which took stock of man's acquisitive passions. "Work with these passions," he advised, "and you can achieve the unbelievable; work against them, and you will have to struggle daily with fresh problems, and to re-learn how shrewd men can be when it comes to circumventing troublesome regulations."[8] The kind of government action

[8] *Ibid.*

which took man's natural instincts into account was exemplified for Rau in the English Poor Law of 1834. In an article on the effects of that law, he hailed the success of the English government in helping men by encouraging them to help themselves.[9]

In Rau's rectoral address at Heidelberg in 1847, he summed up his case against the dangers and inadequacies of government regulation. He observed that liberals were being accused of breaking down society into atoms and corrupting its traditional unity, as if in every age the prosperity of a nation had not depended on the ambition and hard work of its individual citizens. He was alarmed that in their present anxiety some men wanted to abandon all the hard-won liberties of the last few decades and return headlong to a despotic system of rigid planning and controls. Referring to socialist and communist "fantasies," he asked what but naked force would set men to work in a society where private initiative had been abolished along with private property and private enterprise. He admitted that a free economy had its drawbacks — in the autumn of 1847 he could hardly have done otherwise. But the individual's calculation of opportunities and his ambition to seize them were still the most powerful driving forces in society. Where these were exercised freely and with good judgment, society's resources would be put to best use, and its needs would be met most satisfactorily. "Some shocks to the economy are unavoidable whether they result from natural occurrences, or from stoppages of international trade; but just as the trees on the edge of a forest with their stronger roots can better withstand the storm's rages, so a freely growing economy can more easily weather periods of distress."[10]

---

[9] K. H. Rau, "Ueber das englische Armengesetz von 1834 und dessen Wirkungen," *Archiv der politischen Oekonomie*, II (1835), 214–47.

[10] K. H. Rau, *Ueber die Beschraenkungen der Freiheit in der Volkswirtschaftpflege* (Heidelberg, 1847), p. 18.

JOHN PRINCE SMITH

A far more doctrinaire spokesman for free enterprise and free trade than Rau was a young naturalized Prussian who had been trained not within the halls of Halle or Koenigsberg but on the playing fields of Eton and in London warehouses. John Prince Smith (1809–74) was born in London, the son of a lawyer and publicist who in 1817 was appointed to a civil service post in Jamaica.[11] Young Prince Smith was sent to Eton in 1820 but had to break off his education two years later when his father died. During the next nine years he worked at a number of different jobs — as a clerk in a firm of merchants, as a bank clerk, as a parliamentary reporter, and finally as a free-lance journalist in London and Hamburg. In 1831 he was appointed to teach English and French in a secondary school in Elbing, a commercial town in East Prussia second in importance only to the capital of the province, Koenigsberg.

Prince Smith was an indifferent teacher. His students remembered him as tardy, unprepared, and distracted. But he had considerable social success among the merchant class in Elbing, and he began to write articles in German for the local newspaper, the *Elbinger Anzeiger*. These articles were, for the most part, arguments for free trade which just happened to coincide with the views of the Elbing grain exporters who were anxious for free entry into the English market. Because he neglected his teaching duties, and perhaps because his liberal political activities

[11] Biographical data on Prince Smith may be found in Otto Wolff, "Eine Lebensskizze," in John Prince Smith, *Gesammelte Schriften* (Berlin, 1877–80), III, 210–98; *Dictionary of National Biography*, LIII, 86. German usage recognizes the hyphen which Prince Smith added to his name; English usage does not. On Prince Smith's views, see W. O. Henderson, "Prince Smith and Free Trade in Germany," *Economic History Review*, Ser. II, Vol. II (1950), 295–302 [also published in Henderson's *Britain and Industrial Europe, 1750–1870* (Liverpool, 1954)]; Heinrich Herkner, *Die Arbeiterfrage, eine Einfuehrung* (8th ed.; Berlin, 1922), II, 129–36; Julius Becker, *Das deutsche Manchestertum* (Karlsruhe, 1907), a dissertation devoted almost exclusively to Prince Smith's writings of the 1860's.

aroused suspicion, Prince Smith was dismissed from his teaching post in 1840. For six years he stayed on in Elbing writing articles and pamphlets; then he moved to Berlin where he hoped to be offered a position as the editor of a review of economic affairs. In the competition for that job, Prince Smith lost out to another journalist who was a protectionist. He remained in Berlin, joined the German Free Trade Union, and married the daughter of a prominent banker. Free of financial worries for the rest of his life, Prince Smith from 1847 until his death campaigned tirelessly for free trade and made himself Germany's foremost representative of the Manchester school of thought. Not only did he publish books and articles in favor of free trade and free enterprise, but he also carried these ideas into the political arena. From 1862 to 1866, he represented Stettin in the Prussian Diet, and in 1870 he was elected to the Reichstag by the constituency of Anhalt-Zerbst.

As a writer on social and economic questions, Prince Smith is interesting chiefly because of his opportunism. No doubt he came by his opinions honestly; his father before him had written in praise of the natural laws of political economy and in favor of free trade.[12] But social opportunities in Germany reinforced the son's inherited convictions. The rapid rise of this foreigner from an obscure teaching post to the intellectual leadership of powerful commercial interests in Prussia indicates that Prince Smith was a skillful advocate for those interests. Little that he wrote was original or profound. His fundamental ideas were drawn from Adam Smith, although he admitted the influence of Jeremy Bentham and showed some familiarity with the works of Malthus and Ricardo. When he first arrived in Berlin in 1846, Prince Smith spoke of plans to publish a new German edition of *The Wealth of Nations*

[12] In addition to treatises on law, the elder John Prince Smith wrote *Elements of the Science of Money founded on the Principles of the Law of Nature* (London, 1813), and *Advice for the Petitioners against the Corn Bill* (London, 1815).

together with his own commentary on its contents in the light of contemporary experience. These plans never matured, but, in a sense, almost everything he wrote from his earliest forays into journalism to the more substantial works of the 1860's was an application of Adam Smith's principles to the problems of Germany in the mid-nineteenth century.

One of Prince Smith's few original insights into social problems appeared in his first series of articles for the *Elbinger Anzeiger* in September, 1835, in which he discussed the relationship between population curves and wage levels. He was familiar with the Ricardian theory that rising wages promoted population growth, which led to a greater demand for jobs, which in turn drove down wages. But he did not accept the Ricardian conclusion that wages could therefore never rise very far above the level needed for subsistence. Prince Smith agreed: "The measure in which the working class is provided with the necessities of life is governed by the ratio between the number of workers and the demand for their work."[13] But, he pointed out, "in the long run, this ratio is determined by the workers themselves." Prince Smith argued that the workers' notion of what was necessary for existence could be expanded to include what was necessary for a comfortable existence. And if the workers were taught to work for and expect a high standard of living, with attractive housing and clothing and wholesome food, they would postpone marriage until they could provide their families with those comforts. So population growth would be checked and the material welfare of all classes would be enhanced.

The determining condition, then, is always the dominant concept among the working class as to what is necessary for existence. It is, in a word, their level of cultural development. Unfortunately, the views of our countrymen as to what is re-

[13] Prince Smith, *Gesammelte Schriften*, III, 217.

quired for life remains today at a very low level. Depressed as our lower orders are, they lack incentive for hard work.

Dismissing the pessimistic view that population growth would inevitably keep the working class on the verge of starvation, Prince Smith announced in these early articles a theme which he was to enlarge upon later in his career. In April, 1863, Ferdinand Lassalle published a pamphlet entitled *The Open Answer* which restated the Ricardian theory of wages and deplored it as an "eherne oekonomische Gesetz," a phrase often rendered into English as the "iron law of wages."[14] Prince Smith replied to Lassalle and others who were concerned about the future of the German working class by repeating his "golden law of wages," which if brought into operation would eliminate poverty once and for all. Essentially, Prince Smith's message in the 1860's was the same as it had been in the 1830's. Give the working class a strong incentive to save, work hard, and limit the size of their families and the result will be material abundance for society at large.

In the articles of 1835 Prince Smith had noted that the German working classes had a low level of expectation and correspondingly low incentives. In 1839 he published a pamphlet outlining his views on social and economic progress in the future. Despite its title, *Andeutungen ueber den Einfluss des Reichtums auf geistige und moralische Kultur*, the pamphlet did not put forward a materialist interpretation of life, although it did indulge in the grandiose, rather naïve generalizations about history and civilization which were so common at that time in popular writings on social questions. Prince Smith stated that in history men had developed on two levels, the physical and the moral, and that all human development had resulted from the pressure of material necessity. Primitive physical

---

[14] Ferdinand Lassalle, *Gesammelte Reden und Schriften* (Berlin, 1919–20), III, 58–62; John Prince Smith, "Die Sogenannte Arbeiterfrage," *Volkswirtschaftliche Vierteljahrschrift* (1864), 192–207.

needs drove men to exert themselves, and in their struggle to wrest a living from the natural world, their most important faculty had been reason. Reason taught them how to cultivate the soil so they could abandon the life of hunters and food gatherers. After they settled into communities, reason taught them how to protect their property and to keep peace by formulating moral codes and establishing governments. Stagnation did not set in at this agrarian stage of social development because population increases constantly threatened to outrun food supplies, and so men had to learn, again with the help of reason, how to produce more of the necessities of life. By the early nineteenth century, Prince Smith believed, the human race stood on the frontier of a new stage of civilization. New mechanical inventions and the division of labor had so expanded productive capacities that all animal needs could easily be satisfied. Henceforward the driving force in social progress would not be material necessity but divine discontent, a craving for a richer cultural life and for the respect of one's fellow men.

The greatest danger in this new phase of civilization would be the division of society into a few capitalists, on the one hand, and masses of workers, on the other, a division which would be an injustice that might lead to social warfare. "Where industrial advances have brought large numbers of men together, erroneous ideas about society and its relationships threaten the entire social edifice."[15]But the workers must be taught to understand that capital accumulation is required for economic progress and that their very jobs depend upon it; it would be tragic if they put their fallacious and shortsighted notions of what was good for them above the welfare of society as a whole. While the poor are absorbing this lesson, the wealthy must be careful to live modestly and to resist the corrosive influence of money.

[15] *Ibid.*, p. 382.

Prince Smith dealt more pointedly, if less happily, with the problems of poverty and social inequalities in a series of articles published in the *Elbinger Anzeiger* during January and February, 1841. He opened the series under the general title, "Apologie der Gewerbefreiheit," but subsequently renamed it "Ueber die Quelle des Pauperismus." He defined pauperism as "the condition of men . . . whose needs are not in balance with their productivity and who therefore cannot subsist without help from others."[16] His explanations of the causes of pauperism were on a level with his definition. In Prussia the chief cause of poverty, he said, was the fact that millions of thalers were spent to maintain a standing army. Not only did this expenditure waste capital, but it kept thousands of men idle and crippled the country's productive powers. In England, on the other hand, the chief cause of poverty was the English system of poor relief as it had been constituted before the reform of 1834. Prince Smith cited statistics to show that, while the population of England had grown by 30 per cent between 1793 and 1818, English expenditures for poor relief had risen by some 400 per cent, but that after only one year of operation of the reformed system of poor relief, the poor rates had been reduced by 45 per cent.

In view of such unmistakable facts, need anything further be said to prove that pauperism is only the fruit of which poor relief is the seed, and that one grows only in the measure that the other is scattered?[17]

Later in the 1840's when poverty seemed to be spreading in Germany and when social questions were getting more and more attention, Prince Smith was curiously silent on these subjects. He produced at that time a number of studies confined almost wholly to technical problems of banking and credit and to arguments for dropping the barriers to free trade. He touched on social questions only

[16] *Ibid.*, p. 236.
[17] *Ibid.*, p. 239.

in passing. For instance, he argued that free trade would establish international good will and genuine peace, which would lead to a reduction of military budgets which would in turn lead to general prosperity. In 1844 he published his only work in English, a translation of some essays on political economy by a professor at the University of Koenigsberg who was upholding the tradition of Christian Jakob Kraus and Adam Smith.[18] He began to attract attention outside of Prussia; in 1845 one of his pamphlets on free trade provoked a hot retort in Friedrich List's *Zollvereinsblatt*.[19] In 1846, he drew up an "Address to Sir Robert Peel" in which he and a number of Elbing grain exporters hailed Peel's statesmanship in bringing about the repeal of the Corn Laws, a move which caused some stir in both Prussia and Britain. In any case, Prince Smith's prescription for social problems had been clearly stated by the mid-1840's. These problems would resolve themselves, if free enterprise and free trade were allowed to take their natural course. Let governments give businessmen free rein, and business prosperity would benefit all levels of society. The workers should exert themselves, not just to stay alive, but to enjoy a higher standard of life; meanwhile, let them not murmur, like the Jews, while being led into the Promised Land.

HANSEMANN, CAMPHAUSEN, AND BRUEGGEMANN

Not all German businessmen, however, would have accepted Prince Smith as their lawgiver. Some, like Ludolf Camphausen and Karl Heinrich Brueggemann, the editor of the *Koelnische Zeitung*, favored free trade and a highly competitive system but thought that the government should come to the aid of those who were left behind, or

[18] Karl Heinrich Hagen, *Von der Staatslehre* (Koenigsberg, 1839), trans. as *System of Political Economy* (London, 1844).

[19] Friedrich List, "John Prince Smith ueber die Nachteile fuer die Industrie durch Erhoehung der Einfuhrzoelle," *Schriften, Reden, Briefe* (Berlin, 1927–36), VII, 343–56.

trampled, in the rush for profits. Many others, although highly critical of any proposals for government aid to the poor, wanted government aid to business in the form of protective tariffs and subsidies. A representative of the latter point of view was David Hansemann (1790–1864), merchant, insurance magnate, and the most vocal liberal politician in the Prussian Rhineland. Not a theorist, but nevertheless a man of decided opinions, Hansemann owed his prominence to his energy and self-assurance. He was convinced that the welfare of Prussia depended on the welfare of her middle class, on their prosperity and accession to political power. Far from hostile to the working classes, he believed, with Rau, that the best way to help the poor was to give them opportunities for self-help.[20]

A self-made man, Hansemann was born near Hamburg in a little town where his father was pastor. After a brief and irregular education, he moved to Aachen in 1817 when that city was in the throes of an economic crisis. Under the Continental System, Aachen had become the center of a flourishing textile industry; but after 1814, English competition and the general postwar slump forced many mills to close down. This resulted in an extended period of extreme hardship for the workers. Hansemann saw that the system of poor relief then in operation was directed toward helping people out of temporary difficulties, but it did nothing to eradicate the causes of their distress. Although the textile mills gradually resumed work after 1820, Hansemann, who had begun to make money in the wool trade, announced a venture which he believed would improve the lot of the workers by striking at the roots of their trouble. Between 1824 and 1825 he founded the Aachen Fire Insurance Company and provided in its charter that half of

[20] Alexander Bergengruen, *David Hansemann* (Berlin, 1901); Jacques Droz, *Le libéralisme rhénan, 1815–1848* (Paris, 1940), pp. 227–46; Rudolf Haym, *Reden und Redner des ersten preussischen Vereinigten Landtags* (Berlin, 1847), pp. 359–93; Johanna Koester, *Der rheinische Fruehliberalismus und die soziale Frage* (Berlin, 1938), pp. 24–31.

the net profits of the company should be paid over to a Society for the Promotion of Diligence.[21]

Hansemann's fire insurance company became the most important firm of its kind in Germany, and the Society for the Promotion of Diligence flourished with it, although restricted to *Regierungsbezirk* Aachen.[22] The society's activities branched out into several programs to encourage workers to work hard and to save their wages. The very poor were entitled to join a premium savings bank which paid 5 per cent interest on deposits and awarded a premium of three thalers to any depositor who managed to save a total of twenty thalers in the space of three years. For those with larger savings, there was an ordinary savings bank which paid 3½ per cent interest. Between 1837 and 1839, the Society published a fortnightly paper to carry the evangel of the industrial virtues to working-class families. It also operated a number of day nurseries in which by 1844 some 1,139 children of the poor were kept at the nominal monthly rate of two silver groschen per child. Twenty years after its foundation, Hansemann's society was generally regarded as a model for all self-help enterprises.

In 1824 Hansemann had argued with his fellow citizens in Aachen that political issues should not distract them from social reforms "as if one could build the roof of a building without laying its foundation." But after 1830 he became increasingly absorbed in political activity, and his thinking on social problems progressed very little beyond his initial recommendations for self-help. In 1830 the July Revolution in France, the upheaval in nearby Belgium, and some machine-smashing riots in Aachen made him fearful of revolution in Prussia. In December of that year he wrote a long memorandum to King Frederick William

[21] Bergengruen, *Hansemann*, pp. 28–33, 52–55.

[22] J. J. Thyssen, *Darstellung der Einrichtung und der Wirksamkeit das Aachener Verein zur Befoerderung der Arbeitsamkeit* (Aachen, 1845), esp. pp. 1–30.

III to warn him of the danger.[23] The central message of the memorandum was that Prussia should be granted a liberal constitution. But to spur the king to action, Hansemann began by dwelling on the dangers which faced the country: social revolution, political revolution, war, and the decline of Prussian power. He claimed that broadening the base of the Prussian government by guaranteeing equal rights for all and giving political representation to property owners would dispel most of these dangers.

With specific reference to the threat of social revolution, Hansemann said that this was the gravest danger to law and order. He observed that a spirit of rebellion was abroad which sprang from a number of circumstances. One of these was the widespread aspiration for a higher standard of living, a standard out of all proportion to services performed. Another was the growth of industry which had introduced the division of labor and increased the number of men whose livelihood depended entirely on their daily labor. Finally, Hansemann blamed the unrest, in some part, on the high taxes which were levied on basic necessities of life and which were especially onerous to the poor. To dispel the danger of social revolution, Hansemann called on the king to lighten taxes and to foster self-help programs for the working class. Hansemann roundly condemned policies of public assistance or corporate philanthropy as "the most direct and effective invitations to prodigality and sloth." Such policies, he said, encouraged the poor to believe that, no matter how they wasted their lives, society owed them a living. Such policies, then, could only put a heavier and heavier burden on the thrifty and industrious. The lower classes would be debauched, and the whole structure of society would then rot away.[24]

[23] Droz, *Le libéralisme*, p. 228. The text of Hansemann's memorandum to Frederick William III is published in Joseph Hansen, *Rheinische Briefe und Akten zur Geschichte der politischen Bewegung, 1830–1850* (Essen, 1919), I, 11–81. For a condensation of it, see *Unsere Gegenwart und Zukunft*, IV (1846), 106–202.

[24] Hansen, *Briefe und Akten*, I, 12–13.

Hansemann sent this memorandum to Berlin on December 31, 1830, and a few weeks later received a polite acknowledgment from Frederick William III. That the memorandum expressed Hansemann's abiding convictions is indicated by the fact that fifteen years after he wrote it, in 1845, he circulated a copy of it among members of the Rhenish Diet. From the Rhineland a copy was sent to Karl Biedermann, the liberal editor of several publications in Leipzig, who printed a slightly abridged form of the memorandum in his *Unsere Gegenwart und Zukunft.*

During the 1830's Hansemann continued to agitate for a constitution and to look after his business interests. In 1833 he published a political study entitled *Preussen und Frankreich.*[25] In 1838 he was elected president of the Aachen Chamber of Commerce. The accession of Frederick William IV in 1840 wakened hopes for political reform among many Prussian liberals. Hansemann, however, was full of foreboding and set to work on another memorandum which would review political and social conditions in Prussia for the benefit of the new king. In this review Hansemann stated his opinion that the dangers of social revolution had greatly increased in the ten years since he had written his first memorandum. The growth of industry had spawned a large class of men without property, and universal military training had taught them how to organize for the use of force. The continued decline of religion as a force in men's lives, the corruption of morality, and the rise of a "hospital spirit" in the state were corroding the foundations of society. Hansemann was particularly bitter about that "hospital spirit," which led to organized charity for the poor:

Religion and humanity bid us reduce the numbers of the unfortunate among our fellow-men. Here the individual should follow the dictates of his heart in clothing and feeding the poor

---

[25] *Preussen und Frankreich* (2d ed.; Leipzig, 1834) was a blast at the Prussian tax system and created some stir in the early 1830's. See Droz, *Le libéralisme,* pp. 178, 230–31.

and in educating their children. . . . But when the state, or when societies and organizations undertake to support them, the poor come to assume that they have a legal right to help. This undermines morality which from the point of view of civil life consists in diligence, orderliness, thrift, a sensible ambition to increase one's wealth, respect for family ties, and fulfillment of family obligations.[26]

Hansemann seemed to agree with Prince Smith that state aid to the poor intensified the social problem; but he saw nothing objectionable in government measures to foster economic development in general. He advocated a protectionist policy for the Zollverein and in the 1840's conducted a vigorous campaign for government railways. Elected to the Rhenish Diet in 1845, and to the United Diet in 1847, he did nothing to further the tax reforms he had urged upon Frederick William III. Indeed, in June, 1847 he voted against a government bill which proposed to abolish the "mill and slaughter tax," which taxed the poor man's food, and to replace it with a graduated income tax. Nor did he, as Prussian minister of finance from March to September, 1848, do anything to shift the tax burden from the lower classes. Essentially what Hansemann wanted was a social order in which the nobility and middle class would be partners in power, while a sturdy, industrious working class accepted its subordinate position. He foresaw the possibility that the middle class would have to fight the nobility for a share in running the government. In that event he did not want the middle class to be caught in a two-front war with the nobility on the right and the masses on the left. Shrewd as Hansemann was in calculating the political threats posed by social discontent, his assessment of its causes, and his suggestions for measures to relieve it, were altogether ingenuous.[27]

Often allied with Hansemann in the political battles of

---

[26] For the text of the memorandum to Frederick William IV, see Hansen, *Briefe und Akten*, I, 197–268. This memorandum was never sent.

[27] Koester, *Fruehliberalismus*, pp.26–30.

the Prussian Rhineland, Ludolf Camphausen (1803–90) profoundly disagreed with him on questions of social and economic policy.[28] In fact Camphausen, the patrician head of a banking house in Cologne, had so deep an aversion to the *arriviste* from Aachen that he would consent to join the liberal government of Prussia which was formed in March, 1848, only on condition that Hansemann was not to be minister president. The riots in Silesia first kindled Camphausen's interest in the social problem, and although his explanation of the growing distress in Germany in the late 1840's was less doctrinaire and less moralizing in tone than that of Hansemann, it was not much more searching. He told the United Diet in 1847 that the distress resulted from "the growth of the population in a long period of peace, the invention of machines, the introduction of railways, the division of labor, the concentration of labor in factories, and the growing preponderance of capital and credit."[29] Camphausen's belief that industrialization was wrecking human lives reinforced his ambition to see protection not merely dead but damned. Privately and publicly, in the Cologne Chamber of Commerce and in the provincial diets, he denounced tariffs as the means employed by inefficient special interests to make the public pay for their inefficiency. When the protectionists, like Friedrich List, argued that tariffs were necessary for the growth of German industries, Camphausen was among those who replied: "Wir wollen keine Fabriken." Germany would be a happier land if it remained an agricultural country with a few, small domestic industries.

Recognizing that working-class distress could lead to

---

[28] Anna Caspary, *Ludolf Camphausens Leben* (Stuttgart, 1902); Mathieu Schwann, *Ludolf Camphausen* (Essen, 1913); Droz, *Le libéralisme*, pp. 277–313; Haym, *Reden und Redner*, p. 368.

[29] Eduard Bleich (ed.), *Der erste Vereinigte Landtag in Berlin, 1847* (Berlin, 1847), III, 1591; cf. Koester, *Fruehliberalismus*, pp.31–32. For Camphausen's views on free trade, see Caspary, *Camphausen*, p. 78; Schwann, *Camphausen*, I, 201–10, II, 275; Droz, *Le libéralisme*, 277–83. For List's comments, see *Schriften, Reden, Briefe*, VII, 360–82.

social upheaval, Camphausen, after the "potato revolution" of April, 1847, in Berlin, proposed that the government distribute two and one-half million thalers among the eight provinces to be used for the founding of savings banks for workers.[30] These would create a bond of interest between the working class and the government and would lead at once to greater political and social stability. More than that, Camphausen, in the spirit of *noblesse oblige*, called on the upper classes to develop a sense of social responsibility. During the debate on tax reforms at the United Diet in June, 1847, he spoke eloquently in support of the government bill to tax income and reminded his fellow deputies that social justice required some sacrifice on the part of the wealthy.

How obscure and confused are those notions which we associate with the catchwords of our time — words like pauperism, proletariat, communism, socialism, the organization of labor! But this no one will deny — that a truth lies at the base of their shaky exteriors, the truth . . . that every man who is alive has a right to live, and that society must give that right broader recognition. The same principle which condemned slavery as an injustice, the same principle which later declared serfdom an injustice is now pressing forward, and we see it at work in most of the legislative bodies of Europe, and in the spirit of the people. I welcome the law proposed by the government as an expression of that principle, as an expression of social progress. It achieves that fuller recognition of the duty of the property-owner to do something for the man without property.[31]

In 1845 Camphausen was instrumental in bringing to Cologne as editor of the *Koelnische Zeitung* a young publicist who had displayed an enthusiastic interest in promoting both the cause of free trade and the welfare of the lower classes. Karl Heinrich Brueggemann (1810–87), a

[30] Bleich, *Vereinigte Landtag*, II, 136.
[31] *Ibid.*, III, 1591. For an account of the debate on tax reform, see Karl Biedermann, *Geschichte des ersten preussischen Reichstags* (Leipzig, 1847), pp. 336–58. The income tax bill was defeated.

Westphalian, had studied at Bonn and Heidelberg.[32] In later life he confessed that his fundamental ideas on society had changed little since he had read Adam Smith and Ricardo at Heidelberg under the direction of Professor Rau. But the change, though he regarded it as small, was significant. Because he played a leading part in the Hambach Festival, Brueggemann was sentenced to death by the government of Prussia in 1832. This brutal sentence was first commuted to life imprisonment and then after eight years suspended by the grace of Frederick William IV in the year of his accession. While in prison Brueggemann deepened his understanding of the problems of political economy by poring over works of the German philosophers, particularly the works of Immanuel Kant. After his release, he spent several years in Berlin trying, without success, to get a teaching position and writing on political and economic affairs, until at length he was called to the editorial post in Cologne.

During his residence in Berlin, Brueggemann published a book which was conceived as a rebuttal to Friedrich List's *Das nationale System der politischen Oekonomie*. Here Brueggemann defended Adam Smith's free trade theories and cosmopolitan outlook against List's slashing attacks. He met these attacks with the charges that List's economic nationalism was merely selfishness raised to a higher power, and that List's overmastering fear that England would dominate the world with its economy was just a bad dream. Germany, Brueggemann believed, was in a strong position to solve the social problems of the nineteenth century, the problems of industrialization and mass poverty, because Germany had just begun to experience these problems, and because Germans had a firm sense of social responsibility.

[32] *Allgemeine deutsche Biographie*, III, 405; Karl Heinrich Brueggemann, *Meine Leitung der Koelnischen Zeitung und die Krisen der preussischen Politik von 1846–1855* (Leipzig, 1855); Karl Buechheim, *Die Stellung der Koelnischen Zeitung im vormaerzlichen rheinischen Liberalismus* (Leipzig, 1914).

But in working out her solutions, Germany must point the way to other nations and must do so in harmony with them. In this way we shall neither become anglicized, nor will we hate the English, rather we shall within due limits respect their rights and individuality . . . and in the end we shall preserve our own freedom and individuality.[33]

What special preparation did Germany have for the solution of social problems? Brueggemann held that German thinkers had very early seen the dangers inherent in Adam Smith's doctrine of economic individualism. He granted that the doctrine of free competition had served a worthy purpose: historically, it had been a necessary solvent for the feudal-corporative restrictions which were the legacy of the Middle Ages. But the unrestricted activity of individuals pursuing their own interests had its disadvantages, too, and Adam Mueller had been among the first to point these out. All too often free competition led to the exploitation of the weak by the strong; all too often men forgot that true freedom required self-discipline. Not only Adam Mueller, but Immanuel Kant, who was so frequently paired with Adam Smith (although not properly in this case, since Smith did not discuss self-discipline in his writings on economic questions), had emphasized the necessity of moral controls. From teachers like Mueller and Kant, Germans had learned how to be truly free; German workers did not have to suffer the brutal treatment which had been the lot of the English working class; nor would the German upper classes wait until threats of revolution moved them to protect the poor from the rigors of free enterprise.

The Prussian government, for instance, had thought of a Factory Bill for the protection of working-class children as soon as it had thought of factories themselves. And our German conscience finds in this concern, not a limitation, but an affirmation, of our national idea of freedom.[34]

Germany's headstart in solving the social problem was

[33] Karl Heinrich Brueggeman, *Dr. List's nationales System der politischen Oekonomie* (Berlin, 1842), p. 320.

[34] *Ibid.*, p. 92.

the result of her highly developed social conscience, and Germany must set an example to other nations in achieving the "redemption of the proletariat." As a first step in that direction, the workingman must be given back his self-respect. He had a right to a wage which would enable him to live without charitable handouts. An economic system which was in part regulated and in part competitive would allow him to manage his affairs more prudently. He should have membership in a corporate group and, within it, make provision for his children as well as for the poor and the sick. Toward this end, the state should take the lead in founding and administering compulsory sickness funds, widows' funds, and the like, but should give the workers an ever increasing share in their management. Broader educational programs were indispensable for the improvement of the workers' position. But the fundamental problem of political economy was to create a self-supporting, self-regulating citizenry. Germany, which had a strong ethical tradition and which of all European nations had best preserved her economic balance, was already well on the way toward the solution of that problem.[35]

In his defense of free trade, Brueggemann made common cause with liberals like Prince Smith and Rau who believed that the best governed were the least governed. But in advocating an economy which combined a measure of free enterprise with government regulation and corporate security, he joined with those liberals who were prepared to temper their individualist principles. The differences between these points of view appear with particular clarity in the *Staatslexikon*, an encyclopedia of the social sciences published during the 1830's and 1840's, which numbered among its contributors nearly all of the prominent liberal writers of southern Germany.

[35] *Ibid.*, pp. 308–9.

IV

Social Thought in the
Staatslexikon

The *Staatslexikon*, or *Encyclopedia of Political Science*, published by Karl von Rotteck and Karl Welcker during the 1830's and 1840's, was so influential in the development of German liberalism that references to it as a source and repository of liberal ideas have become a ritual observance among historians of the period. Franz Schnabel, for instance, has called it "the fundamental work of pre-March [1848] liberalism, especially in southern Germany."[1] Oscar Stillich and Hans Rosenberg have called it the "standard work" of German liberalism. More recently, Hans Kohn has observed that the *Staatslexikon* was "a powerful vehicle for spreading western liberal ideas," Leonard Krieger has called it "the most influential organ of political liberalism in pre-March Germany," and T. S. Hamerow has acknowledged it as "the bible of early liberal thought." If imitation is a form of praise, Friedrich Naumann paid a high tribute

[1] Franz Schnabel, *Deutsche Geschichte im neunzehnten Jahrhundert* (Frieburg im Breisgau, 1929–36), II, 177; Oscar Stillich, *Die Politischen Parteien in Deutschland: Der Liberalismus* (Leipzig, 1911), p. 190; Hans Rosenberg, "Theologischer Rationalismus und vormaerzlicher Vulgaerliberalismus," *Historische Zeitschrift*, CXLI (1930), 526; Hans Kohn, *The Mind of Germany* (New York, 1960), p. 134; Leonard Krieger, *The German Idea of Freedom* (Boston, 1957), p. 315; T. S. Hamerow, *Restoration, Revolution, Reaction* (Princeton, N.J., 1958), p. 63. Naumann's scheme is described in Theodor Heuss, *Friedrich Naumann, der Mann, das Werk, die Zeit* (2d ed.; Stuttgart, 1949), pp. 294–95. Naumann's plans were never realized. On the original work, see also Federico Federici, *Der Deutsche Liberalismus* (Zuerich, 1946), pp. 172–74.

to the *Staatslexikon* just before the outbreak of the First World War when he proposed to bring out a *German Encyclopedia of Political Science.* Naumann hoped, according to his biographer, that this new work would assume "the importance as a moulder of opinion which the *Staatslexikon* of Rotteck and Welcker had had for the generations before and after 1848."

As a reflection of liberal thought on social and economic questions, the *Staatslexikon* presents a multiple image. Sharp differences of opinion and emphasis existed between Friedrich List, who first suggested its publication, and the editors, Rotteck and Welcker. Even more pronounced than the differences of opinion within the first edition was the shift in opinion between the first and second editions (1834–43 and 1845–48 respectively). The emergence of the social problem as a matter of pressing concern in the 1840's led Welcker, who by that time was sole editor, to publish a number of articles dealing with such subjects as "Pauperismus" and "Communismus," which had not been dealt with in the first edition. Indeed, some of the articles printed in the second edition — the one on the food shortage of 1847 is a good example — were so topical that they seem to have been written for a magazine rather than for a scholarly reference work. The contributors of these articles were not all "dualistic" liberals like Rotteck and Welcker, who advocated radical measures toward moderate goals.[2] Some were out-and-out radicals — some, even extremists — whose views were almost indistinguishable from those of contemporary socialists. Although all of the new contributors of the 1840's had been persecuted in some way for their views, although all of them favored a diminution of the police power of the state, they did not hesitate to call for government intervention in economic affairs in the interests of social welfare. Where the original editors, Rotteck espe-

[2] The term "dualistic" is from Krieger, *The German Idea of Freedom*, p. 242.

cially, had emphasized the responsibility of the individual for his own well-being and had argued the sanctity of private property, the new roster of contributors emphasized the responsibility of the state for its citizens and argued the tyranny of wealth.

FRIEDRICH LIST

In April, 1833, Friedrich List (1789–1846) suggested the compilation of the *Staatslexikon* to Rotteck and Welcker, who because of their radical journalism had been dismissed from professorships at the University of Freiburg.[3] List wanted to bring out an encyclopedia which would make available to the general reader the growing body of information and ideas in the fields of political science, history, and economics, in order to break the monopoly of this knowledge possessed by academicians and government experts. Although they had to put aside other projects already begun, Rotteck and Welcker acted on List's suggestion, and the first volume of the encyclopedia was published in 1834. Progress thereafter was slow; it was interrupted by quarrels between List, who wanted short, readable articles calculated to stir up German national sentiment, and Rotteck and Welcker, who tended to write and commission scholarly articles dealing primarily with constitutional issues. After Rotteck's death in 1840, List broke off all connection with the work, and Welcker, toiling on alone, brought the first edition to completion. Then, because of its enormous popular success, he supervised the publication of an enlarged and revised second edition.

Before disowning his brain child, List contributed several articles to the *Staatslexikon*, articles which clearly reflect the ideas of a man who deserves attention in any discussion of the views of German liberals on social questions. It is true that after 1830 List could hardly be called a liberal; he seemed to lose all interest in constitutional

---

[3] Hans Zehntner, *Das Staatslexikon von Rotteck und Welcker* (Jena, 1929), pp. 7–26.

questions. And at times he seemed blithely indifferent to social problems. In the Preface to his most important book, he said:

It is unfortunate that the evils which in our day accompany industry have been used as an excuse for rejecting industry itself. There are far greater evils than a class of proletarians: empty treasuries, national impotence, national servitude, national death.[4]

List shouted his message of national strength, national independence, and national survival, not so much as a rabble-rouser, but rather as a man who thinks he is addressing the deaf. And in the course of his obsessive propaganda work he developed an intense concern for the well-being of all classes in the nation and for efficient government direction in every sector of the economy. His tireless agitation had a profound influence on many liberal businessmen who were more interested in national prosperity than in awakening a national consciousness. His attack on the theories of Adam Smith as instruments of English world domination helped to discredit free enterprise ideas in general. And his labors on behalf of railway construction and industrialization led him into explanations of how industry could be developed in Germany without causing the social distress which it had caused in England.

In the articles which List wrote for the *Staatslexikon* in the 1830's, he grew lyrical about man's inventive powers as embodied in the new industrial technology.

[4] Friedrich List, *Das nationale System der politischen Oekonomie* (Stuttgart, 1842), p. lxvii; or *Schriften, Reden, Briefe* (Berlin, 1927–36), VI, 38. List's career is too well known to need recapitulation here; nor have I entered into the controversies over the origins of his ideas and his final vision of a world economy. On these questions, see M. Bouvier-Ajam, *Frédéric List* (Paris, 1938); Friedrich Lenz, *Friedrich List* (Munich, 1936), pp. 282–92; Louis M. Snyder, *German Nationalism, the Tragedy of a People* (Harrisburg, Pa., 1952), pp. 75–100. On List's early liberal views, see Carl Brinkmann, *Friedrich List* (Berlin, 1949), pp. 24–29; for his loss of interest in constitutional issues and for his social views, see Lenz, *List*, pp. 328–29, 376–98.

The power of man is continually growing through new inventions. Just think of the efforts of the handful of men who were responsible for the invention and development of the steam-engine. Not only have these inventors bestowed on small numbers of men power which previously would have required millions of hands, but they have enabled men to dig up the treasures of the earth from its deepest, hitherto impenetrable recesses, to challenge the might of the wind and waves, and to move with the speed of a bird from one place to another. They have increased the welfare, the pleasures, they have renewed the population of the earth, and the beneficent effects of their labor will grow on and on from generation to generation.[5]

In a more sober vein, List pointed out that earlier inventions — the spade, the wheel, the plow, the flour mill — had enabled larger and larger numbers of men to go on living in the same space and at the same time to raise their living standards. He granted that progress had its price and that the introduction of new machines would cause some temporary dislocation. But the long-term advantages would more than compensate for a spell of technological unemployment.[6] He pointed out that the use of steamboats might throw some boatmen out of work, but that it would enormously increase the demand for men in mining and manufacturing. So, too, the division of labor, which was inseparable from the new technology, had its disadvantages. Such specialization was, in fact, the characteristic of a higher level of civilization.

Convinced that new industries were the right Promethean fire for Germany, List ridiculed those Germans who, like Camphausen, were afraid of creating an industrial proletariat. In a letter addressed to King William I of Wuert-

[5] Friedrich List, "Arbeit," *Das Staatslexikon*, ed. Karl von Rotteck and Karl Welcker (2d ed.; Altona, 1845–48), I, 604–9. All subsequent references are to the second edition of the *Staatslexikon*, which reprinted articles from the first edition but which added supplements to the original articles as well as entirely new ones. For List's contributions, see Brinkmann, *List*, pp. 183–91.

[6] Friedrich List, "Arbeit-ersparende Maschine," *Staatslexikon*, I, 610–12.

temberg on April 9, 1843, List urged the king to dismiss such fears and insisted that a proletariat was more likely to appear in an agricultural country which failed to industrialize than in one which harnessed man's new powers. With the growth of the population, as it now goes on from year to year, it is inevitable that the number of men without property will grow in Germany too. Partition of the land has its limits and the cultivation of it can occupy only a limited number of hands. The surplus of men who are capable of work and who must work to eat will seek in the trades what agriculture can no longer provide. The demand for broader activity in manufacturing, for factories, to be precise, will grow louder and more pressing every year. The factories do not give birth to the poor; the poor give birth to the factories.[7]

In List's opinion, England, driving for world monopoly, had industrialized too rapidly and had upset the balance of her economy. In 1841, he claimed, for every two Englishmen in agriculture, three worked at non-agricultural jobs. Also, to undersell all competitors in the world market, English manufacturers had kept wages at the lowest possible levels and had paid no attention to the consequences of this policy for the working class. "The brutalization, the shortages, the distress, the misery of the lower classes, of millions of men, these are the price which England has paid for her industrial monopoly."[8] List harped on this simple interpretation of England's industrial growth in his *Das nationale System der politischen Oekonomie* and in a series of articles and addresses in the 1840's. He also saw in England's industrialization a moral for Germany: Germany must develop an economy which would strike a balance between agriculture, industry, and commerce. German industry would grow steadily and harmoniously in the shelter of a tariff wall which blocked out English competitors. German agriculture could then send excess manpower into the factories and could do away with small, wasteful land-

---

[7] List, *Schriften, Reden, Briefe,* IX, 110.
[8] *Ibid.,* V. 271–72; see also IX, 109–11.

holdings by consolidating them into compact, efficient farms. German commerce would expand, if not overseas on the English model, then overland on the American model. "The lands on the lower Danube, and the Black Sea — the whole of Turkey — the whole southeast beyond Hungary is our hinterland." [9]

List developed his theme — that a balanced expansion of German industry would cure rather than compound social problems in Germany — very cleverly in an article on the Silesian weavers' riots which he published in the *Zollvereinsblatt* in 1844.[10] He held that the distress in Silesia had causes entirely different from the causes of working-class distress in England. The English had adopted machine industry too quickly; Germany had been too slow to do so. Work stoppages in England resulted when the mills produced more than the market could absorb. The Silesians suffered rather from the loss of markets to foreign competition. To restore the Silesian textile industry to health, the government of Prussia should provide it with a secure central European market through tariff protection, and, gradually, mechanical looms should replace hand looms. Diversification of economic interests in Silesia, as existed in the Rhineland, would prevent the return of any such widespread distress in the future.

List, then, was concerned with social problems and eager to improve the lot of the poor. He believed that such improvement would follow inevitably from the expansion of trade and industry and the establishment of a favorable balance between agriculture, industry and commerce. Such developments, however, were national in scope and required a large measure of government assistance. List was not interested in socialist ideas or movements, but he did not hesitate to call upon the state to protect industry, to reorganize agriculture and to create opportunities for com-

[9] *Ibid.*, V, 483–84, 502.
[10] *Ibid.*, VII, 397–403; see also editor's note, VII, 659.

mercial expansion. In one of his articles for the *Staatslexikon*, he hinted broadly that minimum wage legislation would be desirable because it would keep consumer demand at a high level.[11]

KARL VON ROTTECK

Like List, Karl von Rotteck (1775–1840) was an impressario of ideas rather than a creative thinker; and like List he had been dismissed from a professorship because of his political views. But there all similarity between them ends. While List heralded an age of nationalism, Rotteck was an encyclopedist in the tradition of the Enlightenment.[12] Born at Freiburg im Breisgau when that district was still under Habsburg rule, Rotteck grew up in the brave days of Joseph II, the reforming emperor. Shortly after taking his degree in law, he was appointed professor of history at the University of Freiburg and turned to writing history *en philosophe*. In 1812, he began to publish a voluminous history of civilization which became the most widely read work of its kind in the German language.[13] In 1818, he exchanged his chair of history for a chair of political science and, in 1829, brought out the first volume of a students' manual in that field. Specialists, like Rau, found Rotteck's new work amateurish, and the public found it dull. Meanwhile, Rotteck broadened his activities by publishing and writing for popular journals and by entering politics. He was elected to the Diet of Baden, where he became leader

[11] List, "Arbeit," *Staatslexikon*, I, 610.

[12] On Rotteck, see Friedrich Weech, *Badische Biographien* (Heidelberg, 1875-81), II, 211–17; *Allgemeine deutsche Biographie*, XXIX, 385–89; Emil Ganter, *Karl von Rotteck als Geschichtsschreiber* (Freiburg im Breisgau, 1908); Karl Schib, *Die staatsrechtlichen Grundlagen der Politik Karl von Rottecks* (Mulhouse, 1927).

[13] Karl von Rotteck, *Allgemeine Geschichte* (Freiburg im Breisgau, 1812–27). The work went through twenty-five printings by 1867. A review of Rotteck's *Lehrbuch des Vernunftrechts und des Staatswissenschaften* (Stuttgart, 1829–35), by K. H. Rau, appeared in *Archiv der politischen Oekonomie*, III (1838), 398–416.

of the liberal opposition. From the year after his dismissal from Freiburg until his death, work on the *Staatslexikon* claimed most of his time.

The key to Rotteck's liberal views was his concept of *Vernunftrecht*, law based on reason. The faculty of reason, he believed, defines human nature and provides the final sanction for all laws and institutions. Law founded on custom and institutions founded on tradition should be swept away unless they can be re-established on a rational basis. The state has its rational justification in safeguarding the property rights of its citizens, rights which are founded on the law of reason and which existed before the state.[14] To serve its purpose, then, the state must not only guarantee the security of property but must also refrain from infringing on property rights by exorbitant taxes or acts of confiscation. Rotteck conceded that the strict enforcement of property rights had led to some social inequities, that some men luxuriated in riches while others lived in penury. But for the state to violate the sanctity of private property in order to improve the lot of the poor would cause more evils than it would cure. It would kill all initiative to hard work and would thereby cut down productivity. The end result would be poverty for everyone. Social and economic inequalities, he thought, could never be eliminated altogether, but they could certainly be reduced by establishing full equality before the law for all citizens. Let privilege be abolished, let educational opportunities be improved, let business be freed from obsolete restrictions. These reforms would go far toward redressing the balance between rich and poor and preventing a social revolution.

Viewing social problems in the light of *Vernunftrecht*, Rotteck sometimes came close to advancing egalitarian solutions. For instance, in an article on agrarian laws, he began with the premise that inheritance laws have no basis in natural law and should therefore be framed to suit the

[14] Karl von Rotteck, "Eigenthum," *Staatslexikon*, IV, 211–16; Schib, *Grundlagen*, pp. 9–32.

community.[15] The law of entail had once served the interests of the community by giving rise and permanence to a class of wealthy landholders who were independent enough to resist the tyranny of kings and princes and who acted as buffers between the central power and ordinary citizens. But in the future, said Rotteck, resistance to tyranny would be the work of representative bodies elected by the citizens and vested with constitutional rights to oppose the government. The law of entail, therefore, no longer served any useful purpose and should be abolished. On the other hand, laws which allowed the free divisibility of estates should be revised so that land could not be chopped up into plots too small to support a man and his family. This revision would stop the growth of a class of rural day laborers and squatters.

Rotteck also proposed tax reforms to equalize financial burdens. He considered it a cruel injustice to force a peasant to pay taxes on land which he worked for a living while investment capital remained tax-free. All sources of income, he said, should be taxed, and his answers to objections put forward by the capitalists are a good example of his whole approach to political and social problems.

In conclusion, one general remark: The most important opponents of a tax on capital are the capitalists themselves, and their judgment in this respect seems to be warped, and their ardor insincere. Their opinions, accordingly can not be decisive in political questions which should be based on . . . the law of reason. Interests always come into conflict; truths, never. The tax on capital is required by justice and by political wisdom. To overcome the difficulties and set aside the inconveniences connected with it is a problem for applied finance.[16]

The state, in Rotteck's view, should reform its laws governing the inheritance of property and the taxation of property. But what should it do for those who had no property?[17]

---

[15] Rotteck, "Agrarische Gesetze," *Staatslexikon*, I, 401–6.

[16] Rotteck, "Capital–Steuer," *Staatslexikon*, III, 52.

[17] Rotteck, "Armenwesen," *Staatslexikon*, I, 670–79.

He acknowledged that the state, no matter how its purpose was conceived, must concern itself with the problem of poverty. If the end of the state was conceived as the promotion of the general welfare, it followed that care of the poor was a direct responsibility of the state. And if the end of the state was conceived as the protection of property, then care for the poor was an indispensable means of removing threats to property owners. Rotteck, however, defined responsibility for the poor only in the most general terms. The duty of the state to promote the general welfare was fulfilled by clearing away obstacles to economic growth and encouraging all citizens to be prosperous. The state could not claim to be promoting the general welfare when it enacted laws which forced one man to support another or favored one class over another. Moreover, the duty of the state to protect property invested property owners, but not the poor, with rights. The poor, therefore, had no legal claim to state aid, and that was as it should be. For, with the knowledge that they have no right to expect help, the poor would work harder and would plan for their future. Where extraordinary distress occurred, the state should encourage self-help associations and private charities to take care of the distressed. If these organizations proved inadequate, their efforts could be supplemented by community action. Only in those exceptional cases in which local communities could not cope with the problem should the central government take charge.

KARL WELCKER AND THE SECOND EDITION

The sole editor of the *Staatslexikon* after 1840, Karl Theodor Welcker (1790–1869), was another academician turned politician and publicist.[18] A native of Hesse-Darmstadt,

[18] On Welcker, see Karl Wild, *Karl Theodor Welcker, Ein Vorkaempfer des aelteren Liberalismus* (Heidelberg, 1913); Wilhelm Erhard, *Die Grundlagen der Staatslehre Carl Theodor Welckers* (Wuerzburg, 1910). An unfinished work by Welcker was *Das innere und auessere System der praktischen natuerlichen und roemisch-christlich-germanischen Rechts-*

Welcker attended the universities of Heidelberg and Giessen and began teaching at the latter in 1813. During the next ten years he taught briefly at Kiel, Heidelberg, and Bonn. While at Bonn, Welcker was tried, along with Ernst Moritz Arndt, on charges of "demagoguery." After his acquittal he went to the University of Freiburg as professor of jurisprudence. Dismissed in 1833, he was reinstated briefly in 1840 only to be dismissed again in 1841. Welcker was somewhat luckier in his political career. He was elected to the Diet of Baden in 1831 and to both the *Vorparlament* and the National Assembly at Frankfurt in 1848. Looked upon as a dangerous radical before 1848, Welcker in later life was considered sufficiently respectable and trustworthy to represent the Grand Duchy of Baden on diplomatic missions to Sweden and Austria-Hungary. After 1833, the *Staatslexikon* became the focus of his literary activity, and a grandiose work which he had begun in the 1820's never reached completion.

Fundamentally, Rotteck and Welcker agreed with each other on political questions; both held the contract theory of the state and both campaigned for constitutional government and civil liberties. But in their many years of collaboration in the Baden Diet and on the *Staatslexikon*, certain differences emerged.[19] Rotteck admired the logic and revolutionary zeal of the French; Welcker was more impressed by the moderation of the English and found in English history the free development of the Germanic tradition of popular participation in government. While Rotteck appealed to *Vernunftrecht* as the sovereign guide to conduct, Welcker appealed to *Sittenrecht*, the moral law. Whereas

---

Staats- und Gesetzgebungslehre, Vol I (Stuttgart, 1829). Only the first volume appeared.

[19] Wild, *Welcker,* pp. 147–48, 172; Welcker, "Karl von Rotteck," *Staatslexikon,* XI, 629–65. For Welcker's views on the moral role of the state, see his articles "Eudaimonismus, Egoismus, Epikuraeismus, Individualismus," *Staatslexikon,* IV, 52–53; and "Gesammtwohl," *Staatslexikon,* VI, 621–24.

List had thought of the state as the organizing agency of a national community and Rotteck had thought of it as a convenient body for the safeguarding of individual rights, Welcker thought of it rather as a moral entity. As such, the state must promote the general welfare in the sense that it promotes the moral rather than the material well-being of society. And as one of the guardians of the moral order, the state may make demands on its citizens.

Welcker did not hesitate, for instance, to call for some degree of state supervision of industrial practices. In an article on factory schools, he granted that schools maintained by industrialists for children in their employ could serve a useful purpose, but he insisted that they could not be regarded as substitutes for ordinary public schools. Both the factory owners and the children's parents would be tempted to lengthen the working day to a point where the children would have very little time left for instruction, let alone for outdoor play.

Here the state must intervene on behalf of the children. For the well-being, power, and general development of our nation, even for the progress of agriculture, we should help and encourage industrialization. But we must never sacrifice to it the more important personal development and the health of our fellow-citizens. . . . Because factories have only recently begun to appear in large numbers among us, it is all the easier to make regulations so that industrialists and parents will do nothing to impair the education and health of children.[20]

Welcker's concept of the state as an ethical or moral agency, then, carried him somewhat further than Rotteck in advocating government intervention in economic and social problems. The social pressures of the 1840's were also an important influence in this direction. When Rotteck died, socialist and communist movements were virtually unknown in southern Germany. Welcker, however, thought he saw them gaining in strength as social conditions

[20] Welcker, "Fabrikschulen," *Staatslexikon*, IV, 576.

worsened after 1844, and his forebodings emerge clearly in the second edition of the *Staatslexikon*. In an article especially prepared for that edition, he remarked that the liberal principle of individualism had been identified with egotism and naked self-seeking and had become difficult to defend. Some men were so disgusted with the spectacle of this false individualism that they wanted to "abolish it by making everything — rights, property, family — common to everyone."[21]

In his article on individualism, and again in a special supplement to Rotteck's original article on property, Welcker alluded to communist and socialist attacks on the principle of private ownership and remarked that the time had come for a restatement of the rights of the individual to own material goods.[22] God and nature, he said, created men with individual bodies and, consequently, with individual material needs. Just as the body is necessary for the human soul, so private property is required for the development of the free legal personality. A man who is not entitled to own the means of his livelihood, a man who depends on someone else for his subsistence, can never be free in any meaningful sense of the word. Private property rights are prerequisites of civil liberty, and the state is bound by the law of God and of nature to guarantee those rights. But in view of the growing attack on property, the state must make clear that no one has the right to acquire or hold property by inequitable inheritance laws, unjust tax exemptions, or obsolete privileges.

There is only one safeguard against the vandalism and despotism which are threatened by the lying deeds and the plundering, levelling passions of communism. That safeguard lies in the broader realization of those eternal principles of justice, and the application of them to present-day conditions.[23]

[21] Welcker, "Eudaimonismus . . .," *Staatslexikon*, IV, 522.
[22] Welcker,' 'Eigenthum: Nachtrag," *Staatslexikon*, IV, 216–17.
[23] *Ibid.*, p. 217. See also Welcker's "Nachtrag" to Rotteck's "Capital-Steuer," *Staatslexikon*, III, 53–64.

Welcker's anxiety over social problems in the 1840's moved him not only to restate his own and Rotteck's position on them but also to have several articles especially written for the *Staatslexikon* by a number of new contributors. One of these was Gustav von Struve (1805–70), a Mannheim lawyer with side interests in vegetarianism, phrenology, and radical journalism. In 1845 Struve was jailed briefly for calling Metternich a traitor; in 1848 he was to win a certain kind of fame as the leader of the republican movement in Baden. He contributed to the second edition of the *Staatslexikon* an article on the proletariat which was bitter and impassioned. Defining the proletariat as a class of workers who own no property, he argued that in every well-run state a member of the proletariat could earn enough in one year to become a property owner. Further, in every well-run state, all men began life as members of the proletariat. Obviously, Struve found his model of a well-run state in the New World. Europe, he said, ground down its poor with unjust taxes, compulsory services, and military training. In Germany the proletariat could no longer earn enough to sustain life. "One must be very short-sighted to believe that this is the result of a year's bad harvest. The shortage of foodstuffs in Germany is rather the result of our political conditions . . . ."[24]

Counting all journeymen, factory workers, and rural day laborers among the proletariat, Struve arrived at the fantastic estimate that three out of every four Germans belonged to this class.

Struve's view of the problem was more desperate than his remedies. How could the lot of the proletariat be improved? That question, he said, was the great question of the day, and Europe must find an answer or lapse into bar-

[24] Gustav von Struve, "Proletariat," *Staatslexikon*, XI, 212. On Struve, see *Allgemeine deutsche Biographie*, XXXI, 676–87; *Dictionary of American Biography*, XVIII, 158–59; Gustav von Struve, *Diesseits und Jenseits des Oceans* (Koburg, 1863).

barism while the further progress of civilization passed over to America.

The evil which underlies the misery of our proletariat may be characterized as the reverse of that evil which corrupts our upper classes. Our princes, nobles, and lords, our higher dignitaries of church, state, and army, have too much; our proletariat has too little. It comes down to this: some of the superfluous riches and educational advantages of these classes must be taken away and bestowed upon the proletariat.[25]

After his wild language, Struve's specific proposals for the redistribution of wealth were rather tame. He called for revision of inheritance laws so that estates could be divided equitably. He favored the abolition of guilds and the substitution of free associations of workers. He demanded freedom of the press, of conscience, and of learning. He called for the abolition of upper-class privileges and the dissolution of the standing armies of soldiers and bureaucrats. His article was less remarkable for its recommendations than for its incendiary tone.

Another new contributor to the second edition of the *Staatslexikon* was Karl Mathy (1806–68), a lawyer and liberal government official in Baden who lost his job in 1834 because he had taken part in the Hambach Festival.[26] Mathy spent the late 1830's teaching school in Switzerland and writing articles on Swiss political institutions for Rau's *Archiv der politischen Oekonomie*. He returned to Baden in 1840, reentered politics, and began writing for the *Staatslexikon*. In an article on government policy during the food crisis of 1846, Mathy argued against government controls in all except the most extreme circumstances, such as the famine in Ireland in 1845. The government in

[25] Struve, "Proletariat," *Staatslexikon*, XI, 216.
[26] Weech, *Badische Biographien*, I, 45–69; Gustav Freytag, *Karl Mathy* (4th ed.; Leipzig, 1898); E. Angermann, "Karl Mathy als Sozial- und Wirtschaftspolitiker (1842-1848)," *Zeitschrift fuer die Geschichte des Oberrheins*, N.F. LXIV (1955), 492–622.

such circumstances should issue bulletins on food supplies, bring in food from abroad, and provide work for the destitute. But too much should not be expected from government action. The experience of the English government in Ireland proved that

> where a people are so culturally, socially, and economically, backward that they can not find for themselves the energy or the means to improve their lot and help themselves over bad times, they may sink into misery so deep that the most strenuous efforts on the part of the government will be of little avail.[27]

The best way to meet economic and social crises, said Mathy, was not by relying on the government but by voluntary group action. He had high praise for the way in which some communities had responded to the crisis of 1846 by banding together to buy grain or other provisions at wholesale prices and to share in the savings and for those who maintained soup kitchens for the poor and those who opened labor exchanges. In such voluntary action Mathy saw a solution for social problems which were more deepseated than temporary food shortages.

> The spirit of association, if not only directed toward the temporary relief of exceptional distress, but continuously active for the moral training of the working class and above all for redressing the balance between capital and labor, seems destined in our century to give a social character to the forms of political freedom. So the responsibility of the medieval lord to feed his serfs and the responsibility of the corporations for the welfare of their members will be assumed by societies of free and equal men. Times like the present give rise to those principles which will provide social problems with the wholesome solution which they are yet to have.[28]

In contrast to Mathy, Wilhelm Schulz, another newcomer to the *Staatslexikon*'s roster of contributors, made a

---

[27] Karl Mathy, "Fruchtsperre und andere Massregeln gegen die Theuerung im Jahre 1846," *Staatslexikon*, V, 279.
[28] *Ibid.*

strong case for government intervention in economic and social affairs.[29] A guards officer from Hesse-Darmstadt, Schulz, like Mathy, had taken part in the Hambach Festival and had been hounded out of Germany into Switzerland. Early in the 1830's he had become interested in social problems and had read widely in socialist writings. He reacted violently against the socialists but tried to bring other liberals to see what was valid in the socialist critique of liberalism. In the Introduction to a long article on communism which he wrote for the *Staatslexikon* in 1846, he observed, anticipating a famous metaphor, that communism haunted Europe like a spectre but, like most spectres, could not stand the light of day. Its strength, he said, lay in the rise of a proletariat which lived from hand to mouth and whose misery might drive them to social revolution. Europe, he believed, had entered on an era of upheaval. The French Revolution and the wars of Napoleon had awakened men to the possibility of change. The sudden growth of population and the liberal reforms which abolished serfdom and dissolved the guilds had thrown Germany into turmoil.

In Schulz's opinion, as in the opinion of many socialists, those liberal reforms that were based on the principle of free competition were fraudulent. Could the poor compete freely with the rich? Could the uneducated compete freely with the educated?

This so-called free competition which has been so pompously announced as the cure for all pre-existing evils, what is it but the incarnation of the negative spirit, the mere dissolution of long-standing corporative associations which for all their pointless division of work and profit, did nevertheless embody a reciprocity of rights and obligations between members, or at

[29] No biographical notice on Schulz appears in any of the standard reference works. The data here is from Lenz, *List*, pp. 325–26. Schulz's article "Communismus" appears in *Staatslexikon*, III, 290–339. See also Otto Wiltberger, *Die deutschen politischen Fluechtlinge in Strassburg von 1830–1849* (Basel, 1910), pp. 34–35.

least held them together with some permanent interest? Until now only the empty right to work and wages, only the hollow title of free citizen has been conferred upon the poor and uneducated.[30]

Welcker had said that every man must have the right to own property before he can be truly free. Schulz argued that he had to have more than just the right to ownership; he had in fact to be an owner. He suggested that in any genuine system of free competition there had to be some offsetting of handicaps. Society should guarantee to each of its members an education proportionate to abilities and a livelihood proportionate to work done. Every man should be free to rise as high as he could in society, but if he failed, the price of failure should not be starvation.

In the body of his article on communism, Schulz reviewed the history of communist theory and practice from biblical times up to and including the modern German communist movement, which he called a caricature of the French. He then subjected communist proposals for economic, social, cultural, and political reforms to a searching examination, in the conclusion of which he asserted that men must have freedom to express their individuality and to be themselves because human nature demanded that freedom. He accused communist writers of doctrinaire arrogance and, among German communists, distinguished two groups. On the one hand were those who were well-meaning but muddleheaded; on the other hand were those loud, clever, men who themselves wanted to exploit the suffering of the masses and who had already become agents of antiliberal reaction. Schulz repeated his prescription for the social problem in an article on Fourier. While dismissing Fourier's ideas as grotesque although honoring his motives, Schulz reasoned that society should guarantee a suitable education for all young people and a minimum livelihood for all adults. All that was required to accom-

[30] Schulz, "Communismus," *Staatslexikon*, III, 292–93.

plish these two simple goals was a series of co-ordinated laws and regulations.

The initiative for these laws and regulations can come only from the state which represents society in its unity. So we see how we are again and again brought back from the field of socialism into the field of politics.[31]

ROBERT VON MOHL

Another contributor to the *Staatslexikon*, Robert von Mohl (1799–1875), agreed with Schulz that government action was essential to social reform but went well beyond Schulz in suggesting measures which the government should take.[32] Descended from an old "Beamtenfamilie" in the service of Wuerttemberg, Mohl studied law at Tuebingen, Heidelberg, and Goettingen, and in 1824, at the age of twenty-five, was appointed professor of political science at Tuebingen. In 1845 his activities during an election campaign displeased the government at Stuttgart, and he was demoted from his professorship to an administrative post at Ulm. Two years later he was called to Heidelberg, where, like his colleague Karl Heinrich Rau, he divided his energies between academic work and political action. In 1848 he was a member of both the *Vorparlament* and the National Assembly in Frankfurt, associating in the Assembly with the left-center group. From August, 1848, to May, 1849, he was minister of justice in the Assembly's shadow government. At the age of sixty Mohl quit teaching to act as a diplomatic representative for the grand duchy of Baden at Frankfurt and later at Munich. The year before his death, he was elected to the Reichstag as a Liberal.

Mohl wrote a great many articles for the *Staatslexikon*, most of them on technical subjects such as prison adminis-

---

[31] Schulz, "Fourier," *Staatslexikon*, V, 28.

[32] Robert von Mohl, *Lebenserrinerungen, 1799–1875* (Stuttgart, 1902); Karl Friedrich, *Heidelberger Professoren aus dem neunzehnten Jahrhundert* (Heidelberg, 1903), I, 272–75; Weech, *Badische Biographien*, III, 85–109.

tration, police organization, provisions for better sanitation, and the like. One article, however, which he wrote jointly with Karl Mathy for the second edition, surveyed broader problems.[33] It was in large part a condensation of an earlier article which he had published in Rau's *Archiv der politischen Oekonomie* in 1835. And it was a terminal point in a long train of thought which, for Mohl, had begun in an early study of the mechanics of government administration.

Mohl was a lawyer by training and temperament. A somewhat neglected figure in the history of nineteenth-century liberalism, he is generally associated with the concept of the *Rechtsstaat*, which he did so much to propagate. His first major publication was a study of the constitution of Wuerttemberg; his second was a survey of government operations.[34] In the latter, his method was to proceed by way of definitions and distinctions to stake out different areas of government responsibility and to describe the workings of the appropriate agencies. The results of this quasi-scholastic method were often disappointing. For instance, when discussing government policies on population control, Mohl merely rehashed the ideas of Malthus and concluded lamely that since rapid population change would affect the well-being of society, governments must take steps to check both rapid growth and rapid decline. Where Prince Smith and Rau and, to some extent, List had offered insights into the economic consequences of population growth, Mohl offered none. But his method had strengths as well as defects and on one important problem — the problem of poverty — carried him into a far deeper and more subtle treatment than that of those writers whose interests were primarily economic.

[33] Karl Mathy and Robert von Mohl, "Gewerbe-und Fabrikwesen," *Staatslexikon*, V, 738–80.

[34] Robert von Mohl, *Staatsrecht des Koenigreiches Wuerttemberg* (Tuebingen, 1829–31); and *Die Poliezei-Wissenschaft nach den Grundsaetzen des Rechtstaates* (Tuebingen, 1832). For Mohl's views on the population problem, see *Polizei-Wissenschaft*, I, 72–93.

Many liberals — for instance, Prince Smith, Hansemann, and Rotteck — regarded poverty as an individual problem to be relieved chiefly by individual self-help; others — for example, Rau — considered it an abnormal condition, the result of some natural mishap, like drought, or of some temporary aberration in the economy, like overproduction. Mohl, making his legalistic distinctions, pointed out the difference between individual poverty and mass poverty, between poverty which is accidental and that which results from the way in which society is organized.

Essentially different from the kinds of poverty which affect individuals and have particular causes is that poverty which grips whole classes of society and which is not the fault of any one individual or the result of extraordinary circumstances, but is rather the consequence of the whole structure of the relationship between capital and income in that sector of society.[35]

Mass poverty of that kind, said Mohl, created a distinct social class, a proletariat. He thought it likely that all human societies have had and would continue to have their poor. But not all societies have produced a proletariat, and with reasonable safeguards, no society needed to do so.

In dealing with individual poverty, Mohl, like Rau or Rotteck, recommended that the government help the poor to help themselves. For idlers and spendthrifts, he suggested remedial schooling and compulsory workhouses. To offset accidental loss of property or income he recommended insurance schemes, the provision of government credit in the form of low-interest loans, and government encouragement of savings banks and of benevolent associations with special relief funds. The state could also help impoverished families by making it possible for them to emigrate or to resettle in "poor colonies" on unused land in their native countries. The state would lease land and

[35] Mohl, *Polizei-Wissenschaft*, I, 416–17. The importance of Mohl's distinction is noted in Goetz Briefs, *The Proletariat* (New York, 1937), pp. 63–64.

buildings to the resettled colonists and would give them a start by supplying them with the necessary tools and livestock.[36]

Mohl, however, saw clearly that self-help measures, even with government encouragement, were no remedy for the mass poverty of either a rural or an urban proletariat. The poor farmer whose plot was too small to support him or his family might try to improve his condition by leaving the land; but a movement of poor country dwellers into the towns would only shift the scene of misery and increase the numbers of the urban proletariat unless society itself took preventive action. The factory workers and artisans in the towns were as powerless as the poor villagers to help themselves. Few, if any, of the urban poor could ever expect to own their own factories or small businesses.

The necessary capital is much too considerable for the worker to earn, even by the hardest work and with high wages. As a rule, too, he lacks the necessary versatility and the required business connections. The best fate which can befall him is to have continuous employment in his subordinate position; but even this will be denied him by illness, old-age, trade crises, and the introduction of new machines. Often thousands, perhaps hundreds of thousands, will suddenly be deprived of their income until the market improves, or they remain condemned to a competitive struggle which grows more hopeless every day . . . until they go under.[37]

To improve the lot of the urban proletariat, Mohl proposed four kinds of government action.[38] The most drastic of these was his first proposal that the state should try to fix minimum wages. Industries should be given every possible assistance, including tariff protection, in order to make maximum profits. The government might then with

[36] Mohl, *Polizei-Wissenschaft*, I, 339–79.
[37] *Ibid.*, pp. 421–22.
[38] *Ibid.*, pp. 430–47.

perfect justice direct the industrialists to pay their workers a fair share of the profits. Mohl also proposed that the government do everything in its power to prevent work stoppages. He admitted that some business depressions were probably unavoidable, but the government could then help the workers over their periods of unemployment with measures such as group savings plans. Finally, Mohl urged the government to try to lessen class hatred and to uphold moral standards among the workers. As means to these ends, the government should see to it that the churches ministered to the needs of the working class and that the workers were provided with suitable shelter either through a ban on jerry-building or through government subsidies for workers' housing projects.

Having outlined the problems of the proletariat and suggested solutions for them in his *Polizei-Wissenschaft,* Mohl enlarged on these themes in a long article published in 1835 and later condensed for publication in the *Staatslexikon.* Here he listed the evils which the workers suffered: the decay of family life, the lapses into alcoholism and sexual promiscuity, the exploitation of workers, especially in the provision of miserable housing, the destruction of the workers' pride resulting from their dependence on state aid, the physical damage done to them by long hours of work under unhealthy conditions. Many of these evils he knew at secondhand from his reading of reports on working-class conditions in England. He warned his readers of the dangers to society when any significantly large section of it is so exploited and depressed. The least of these dangers was that the proletariat would demand a redistribution of wealth through direct or indirect taxes. More frightening was the danger of attacks on property in outbreaks of crime or of attacks on law and order in revolutionary movements.[39] These evils and dangers had

[39] Robert von Mohl, "Ueber die Nachteile welche sowohl den Arbeitern selbst, als dem Wohlstande und der Sicherheit der gesammten buerger-

appeared first in England with the spread of new industry. Belgium and France had begun to experience them, and Germany, especially since the formation of the Zollverein, was beginning to show the same symptoms. It was imperative for the German governments to find means to dispel these evils and to preserve social peace.

But this can hardly be done without a fundamental reordering of the whole social structure and therefore it is fallacious to hold with MacCulloch the . . . comfortable opinion that what others do to improve the position of the workers is trifling compared to what the workers can do for themselves. Here, if anywhere, help from the highest government authority is essential.[40]

Mohl classified the means already proposed by others for counteracting the baleful effects of industrialization under five headings.[41] First there were proposals which mistook the cause of the evils, for example, those which called for a return to guild regulations or, conversely, for an extension of *Gewerbefreiheit*. Both of these proposals, although they contradicted each other, misconstrued social history. The dissolution of the guilds was not, in Mohl's opinion, a cause of industrialization; it merely hastened the process. More *Gewerbefreiheit* would hardly remedy the ills of industrialism; a return to guild regulation would be comparable to committing suicide to cure a disease. Another class of proposals treated the symptoms rather than the disease. These were the suggestions for such things as savings banks, disaster funds, and day nurseries for the workers' children. All of these were useful but inadequate. Still another class of proposals aimed at

lichen Gesellschaft von dom fabrikmaessigen Betriebe der Industrie zugehen, und ueber die Nothwendigkeit gruendlicher Vorbeugungsmittel," *Archiv der politischen Oekonomie*, II (1835), 141–203.

[40] *Ibid.*, pp. 158–59. Mohl's reference is evidently to John Ramsay MacCulloch, *Treatise on the Principles, Practice, and History of Commerce* (London, 1831).

[41] Mohl, "Ueber die Nachteile," pp. 159–73.

raising wages by diminishing the number of workers. Mohl thought that cutting down the number of job-seekers probably would bring a temporary rise in pay but would hardly affect other evils such as periodic unemployment, unhealthy working conditions, and the workers' loss of independence. A fourth class of proposals included those which Mohl considered contrary to law, morality, and religion. He cited, as an example, a scheme to make the industrialists buy their workers as slaves. The industrialists would then be forced to protect their investment and would see that their slaves were well fed and well housed. In the final category, Mohl lumped together all those schemes which he considered contrary to human nature, among them the schemes of Fourier and Saint-Simon.

Mohl believed that his own solution for the problems of industrialism went to the crux of the matter.[42] The worst evil, in his opinion, was not the workers' poverty, but their sense of futility. The first step in any program of social reform must be to restore to the workers their self-respect and to offer them hope for the future. To restore their self-respect, the government must outlaw every form of exploitation: the sweating of children, the driving down of wages, the truck system, company stores, excessively long working hours. Employers might complain that higher wages and shorter working hours would price their products out of the market, but they would soon find out how a well-paid working class would swell the demand for manufactured goods. To put an end to class hatred workers should be brought into profit-sharing plans which, if broad enough, would create a community of interest between capital and labor.

To offer the workers some hope for the future the state should give them an opportunity to achieve economic independence.[43] Most of them lacked the training and money

[42] *Ibid.*, pp. 173–85.
[43] *Ibid.*

to strike off on their own; the state should help them to overcome these handicaps. Schools for the training of skilled workers would be comparatively easy to set up; but to supply the workers with the capital they would need to establish their own businesses would be difficult. Mohl advocated a program of government loans to carefully selected workers, which would enable them to be their own masters. Certainly only a few would achieve this independence, but the fact that it could be done by the more intelligent and enterprising members of the working class would be a source of encouragement to the general run of workers. Finally, Mohl called for measures to improve the spiritual and physical condition of the workers. Some such improvements, he thought, would follow naturally from the restoration of their self-respect. Segregation of the sexes in factories, tract societies, and missions might check the spread of immorality, but Mohl warned against expecting too much from endeavors of that kind. Industrial work, like any other kind of work, had its characteristic disadvantages. It was routine and confining, and no amount of effort could make it otherwise. Improvement could and should be made but not in the false hope of eliminating the evils of industrialism altogether.

Before summarizing Mohl's earlier arguments for government controls of industry and for aid to the working class, the article by Mathy and Mohl on "Gewerbe- und Fabrikwesen" in the *Staatslexikon* raised some fundamental questions of social policy. The first section of the article might have been written by Friedrich List in a moment of calm. It urged the importance of industrialization for the development of a strong nation. Just because Germans dreaded the consequences of industry as they had appeared in England, they should not resign themselves to the fate of such backward countries as Portugal, Spain, and Naples. Germans could learn from England's mistakes;

they could avoid both overcommitment to industry and the brutalization of the workers. In the next section of the article, referring to *Gewerbefreiheit*, the authors posed the crucial issue of social liberalism: freedom versus regulation. Here they stated a basic principle to which all good liberals could subscribe.

Freedom is the natural condition; it is a right which needs no particular justification; limitations on freedom, on the other hand, must be proved to be necessary for the maintenance of the rights of others or for the higher purpose of the entire community.[44]

The third section of the article repeated Mohl's opinions on what measures governments could take to help the working class, measures which were considerably broader than many liberals would have thought necessary for the "higher purpose of the entire community." The concluding sections pleaded for protective tariffs and working-class education.

Mohl's thinking on social and economic problems was a synthesis of many of the ideas of his liberal contemporaries. Rau's and Prince Smith's views on the necessity of economic progress, List's program of tariff protection, Hansemann's self-help societies, Camphausen's and Brueggemann's affirmation of the responsibility of the upper classes, all these found a place in Mohl's outlook. He agreed in principle with Rotteck and Welcker that the economy should be as free as possible but differed with them on the limits of what was possible. Together with Mathy and Schulz he believed that social distress was less an individual than a collective problem; but more fully than they, he thought out a collectivist solution. In an early passage on government policies, he said:

Laissez faire, laissez passer must not be misunderstood. For it is one thing to interfere at the wrong place, and quite another

[44] Mathy and Mohl, "Gewerbe- und Fabrikwesen," *Staatslexikon*, V, 747.

to offer help where it is needed. A government which, out of laxity or failure of insight, remains completely inactive can do as much harm to the prosperity of the people as one which, with good intentions, acts too vigorously and goes too far.[45]

The question for Mohl was not whether the government should act but rather what should be the direction and extent of government action. In their efforts to find an answer to this question, Mohl and Karl Mathy among the south Germans formulated a program of social liberalism which was to follow a middle course between the extremes of individualism and collectivism. Meanwhile, prominent liberals in Saxony and Prussia were making similar efforts and arriving at similar conclusions.

[45] Mohl, *Polizei-Wissenschaft*, II, 163, n. 2.

V

Social Liberalism

Those liberals who, together with Mohl, favored a program of government action to relieve the distress of the proletariat found themselves exposed to critical attacks from three directions: liberal, conservative, and socialist. Many of their fellow liberals, like Rau, maintained that the hardships of the 1840's were little more than growing pains and that it would be foolhardy to rush into long-range reforms to correct temporary conditions. The conservatives professed to see a logical inconsistency in the efforts of the social liberals to compromise, without surrendering altogether, their individualist principles. And most socialists, agreeing on this point with the conservatives, scoffed at men who were ready to tinker with economic controls and social reforms but were blind to the necessity for overhauling the social structure from top to bottom.[1] To defend their position, then, the advocates of social liberalism first had to make their case for restricting free enterprise in the interests of social welfare and, second, had to show why a total surrender to collectivism was unnecessary or undesirable. Finally, they had to establish for themselves a scale of priorities in their reform program: Which should come first — constitutional or so-

---

[1] An interesting expression of this conservative viewpoint may be found in Joseph Maria von Radowitz, *Gespraeche aus der Gegenwart ueber Staat und Kirche* (2d ed.; Stuttgart, 1846), pp. 103–25. For a socialist opinion on the social liberals, see Karl Marx and Friedrich Engels, *Werke, Schriften, Briefe* (Frankfurt am Main, 1927–35), VI, 552.

cial reforms? Three prominent liberals who wrestled with these problems in the 1840's were Friedrich Harkort (1793–1880), Gustav Mevissen (1815–90), and Karl Biedermann (1812–1901).

FRIEDRICH HARKORT

Friedrich Harkort was born in the County Mark, which after 1815 was incorporated into the Prussian province of Westphalia. As a boy, Harkort was trained for a business career and had already been working for several years when, at the age of twenty, he volunteered for military service during the War of Liberation. After his discharge he founded some metallurgical works and, in 1818, set up the first shop in Germany for the manufacture of steam engines and mechanical looms; during the next two decades, he was active in the promotion of steamship and railways companies. Harkort has been called "the most creative and influential of all the German entrepreneurs of his time," but he had little talent for the routine administration of the enterprises he launched and increasingly devoted his time to public affairs.[2] In 1830 and again in 1834, he was a member of the provincial diet of Westphalia; from 1848 to 1873, he represented the town of Hagen, first in the Prussian National Assembly, then in the Erfurt Union Parliament and the Prussian Chamber of Deputies, and finally in the Reichstag. Harkort began early, and continued all his life, to write political commentaries and humorous pieces for local journals. He also turned out a number of pamphlets, some of them promotional, like his *Die Eisenbahn von Minden nach Koeln* (1833), some of them political, like his *Buerger- und*

[2] Fritz Redlich, "Leaders of the German Steam Engine Industry during the First Hundred Years," *Journal of Economic History*, IV, (1944), 129. On Harkort's career, see Louis Berger, *Der alte Harkort, Ein westfaelischen Lebens- und Zeitbild* (Leipzig, 1880); on his social thought, see Hanns Ernst Jansen, *Das Proletariat im Vormaerz in den Anschauungen deutscher Denker* (Kiel, 1928), pp. 73–84.

Bauernbriefe (1851). In other pamphlets he expressed his deep and lasting conviction that the common people had to be prepared for self-government by improvements in public education and in their living conditions.

During the 1840's Harkort published a series of pamphlets which outlined his program for educational and social reforms. The first of these was an effort to focus public attention on weaknesses in the Prussian elementary school system, and to suggest corrective measures.[3] He deplored the narrow curriculum and the low level of instruction which he found in the public schools, and he called for courses in science and history, for vocational training, and for teachers who were better paid and better qualified for their work than those engaged by the government at the time he was writing. He pleaded for government action toward those ends but also proposed to found a "National Society for the Promotion of Elementary Schools and Popular Education" which would enlist all Prussians who shared his concern for improving the schools. Through their association, they would help teachers who were in need, would help keep the school buildings in repair, would foster the publication of popular literature, and would open local libraries.

As a first step toward a national society for promoting educational reforms, Harkort founded a local society at Hagen in 1843 and very rapidly extended its activities to other communities in Westphalia. When the government, apparently resentful of this intrusion of private citizens into government affairs, held up approval of the society's statutes for some eighteen months, Harkort wrote another pamphlet to expose this short-sighted obstruction. Educational reform, he argued, was essential for any solution of the social problem, a problem which menaced the government with revolution. In his initial proposal for reforms

[3] Friedrich Harkort, *Bemerkungen ueber die preussische Volksschule und ihre Lehrer* (Hagen, 1842).

he had warned that the rapid changes of the past few generations had cut social and religious ties which for centuries had given men status, a sense of security, and a goal in life. Broken loose from those ties, men were falling into an insecure, restless mass which threatened to overthrow what was left of the social order. Educational reform could help avert this threat in two ways. By providing vocational training in public schools, the government could give the workers that security which comes with the mastery of a skilled trade. And by inculcating in the workers a respect for immaterial, cultural values, it could innoculate them against "materialistic communism."[4]

Harkort's most general discussion of social reform appeared in his pamphlet, *Bemerkungen ueber die Hindernisse der Zivilisation und Emanzipation der untern Klassen,* which is not only an important document in the history of social liberalism but an appealing tribute by this self-taught man to the values he wanted to instil into the working class.[5] The pamphlet begins with a sweeping review of human progress, which is defined as growth in knowledge, or "conquests of the mind." Progress has been retarded by the fact that most of mankind has been kept in darkness; from the civilization of ancient Egypt to that of medieval Europe, knowledge had been a monopoly of the priests and the nobility. The invention of the printing press and the Protestant movement might have broken the monopoly. But from the sixteenth to the eighteenth century the energies of Europe were diverted into religious wars and petty controversies, into the creation of despotic governments, and into the maintenance of standing armies. For these sins, Europe had been visited with the

[4] Friedrich Harkort, *Geschichte des Vereins fuer deutsche Volksschule und fuer Verbreitung gemeinnuetziger Kenntnisse* (Elberfeld, 1845), p. 3.

[5] Friedrich Harkort, *Bemerkungen ueber die Hindernisse der Zivilisation und Emanzipation der untern Klassen* (Elberfeld, 1844). Page references are to a second printing with an introduction and notes by Julius Ziehen, published at Frankfurt am Main in 1919.

French Revolution and the wars of Napoleon; in the aftermath of those disorders, the governing classes had regained power while the people sank back into ignorance and helplessness. Unable to earn a decent livelihood or to acquire property by hard work, these people were ready to seize property by force. Unable to distinguish between false and true prophets, they were ready to follow any leader who promised them a better life.

What could be done to redeem civilization before a wave of revolutions destroyed it? Harkort's answer led him to examine one after another the different social problems which affected the rural and urban populations. In the country, he said, the crux of the problem seemed to be overpopulation.

An apparent surplus of men flows from the country into the towns, and there, by excessive competition they drive down wages, and swell the numbers of the homeless, while at home, with better cultivation, there would be space and income for all.[6]

If the farming classes were taught soil chemistry, new methods of cultivation, and the techniques of irrigation as well as reading, writing, counting, and catechism, they could increase the productivity of the land and take a comfortable living from it. Harkort admired the progress which the English had made in agriculture but thought that they had paid a high price for it. He hoped that Germany would not follow the English example in creating large estates and reducing the farmers to the status of wageworkers but would instead maintain an independent class of farmers who owned their land and who had been educated to improve it for themselves.

In industry as in agriculture, new techniques and inventions promised to liberate men from poverty, but instead of becoming servants of the human spirit, they were becoming instruments of subjugation. This perversion of

[6] Harkort, *Hindernisse*, p. 20.

technological progress could be seen most clearly in England, and Germans again should be warned by England's experience. There, large enterprises had been founded with capital which was often acquired through monopolies and questionable deals, even swindles, and these enterprises had driven small competitors out of business. In addition, the introduction of new machinery had resulted in an unprecedented division of labor and had created jobs which required little training or general intelligence. Competition for these jobs by increasing numbers of men, women, and children had reduced wages to a subsistence level. Further, unregulated competition had led to periodic surpluses and gluttings of the market. The mills then shut down and the workers, without reserves to draw on, fell prey to hunger and total demoralization. Historically, the disappearance of the guilds and the lifting of government restraints on business had given a clear field to a class of industrialists who could only be compared to the *condottieri* of Renaissance Italy. Their power depended on their money; they hired mercenaries and used them ruthlessly in a life-and-death struggle with their competitors; they had utter contempt for human rights.

Although I personally am one of the leaders of industry, I despise from the bottom of my heart that creation of value and wealth which is based on the sacrifice of human dignity and the degradation of the working class. The purpose of the machine is to free men from animal servitude, not to fashion a more terrible bondage.[7]

To correct the abuses of modern industry, Harkort advocated government action on several levels. Better education for the working classes was a prerequisite; indeed, the more that man's brute strength was devalued by the introduction of machine power, the more important it would be to develop his intellectual abilities. But education was only a beginning; what was urgently needed was

[7] *Ibid.*, p. 26.

state intervention to guarantee a livelihood to the workers. "If the state can provide security for the masters by means of protective tariffs, then it can do something for their servants as well."[8] The state should forbid child labor during school years and, if necessary, should subsidize parents who depend on their children's wages. The state should limit working hours for all classes of workers and should compel industrialists to help their employees over periods of stress such as those caused by sickness or disability. The state should lighten taxes for the poor by reducing the excise on necessities and increasing it on luxuries. The workers' lot could also be improved by building workers' settlements in the country where they could raise their own food and escape the squalor of urban tenements. Finally, the state should encourage the diversification of industry in any given area, so that a slump in one line of manufacture would not cause unemployment and depression throughout the area.

But not all responsibility for social welfare should be thrust upon the state. Government intervention in the interests of the working classes should be supplemented by the action of private citizens, of the workers themselves, and of members of the upper classes who have a sense of social responsibility. Employers could work out profit-sharing schemes which would be advantageous to them as well as to their employees. Workers could join consumers' co-operatives to protect themselves from the exorbitant charges of retailers. The *Knappschaften*, or unions of German miners, were excellent examples of how the workers could help themselves through group action. The *Knappschaften* had been able to limit working hours in the mines and had an admirable program of sickness and disability insurance. Collective measures by such voluntary associations would be the best answer to socialist schemes for an enforced collectivism. Harkort reviewed

[8] *Ibid.*, p. 28.

the socialist projects of Babeuf, Cabet, Saint-Simon, Fourier, Owen, and Weitling and concluded: "All these doctrines and systems come to grief on the inviolability of private property and the sanctity of marriage, or on the freedom of the mind."[9] The proletarian did not really want state ownership of property; he only wanted a little property for himself. He did not want to live under rigid state discipline but rather to enjoy a certain minimal security together with the greatest possible social and intellectual freedom.

In still another pamphlet, Harkort explained where the different kinds of social action which he recommended could be most effectively applied.[10] State aid, he believed, was a crying necessity for the very poor — some 276,000 families in Prussia — who needed government loans for resettlement and training for new jobs as well as relief money to allow them to live decently until they found a steady source of income. The moderately poor, whose numbers he estimated at 750,000 families, those who had just enough in good times to make ends meet, should be compelled, or encouraged, to join associations which would help them weather bad times. The well-to-do and the wealthy should recognize both the opportunity and the danger which were theirs; above all, they ought to take the lead in solving social problems by voluntary group action. Harkort suggested the immediate founding of agricultural societies, societies for public education and the dissemination of useful knowledge, reading societies, health insurance plans, savings banks, employment offices, and societies for the care of homeless children and other unfortunates. Such collective action freely undertaken, would knit society together and would obviate any need for the system of iron regulation which the socialists were demanding.

[9] *Ibid.*, pp. 44–45.
[10] Friedrich Harkort, *Die Vereine zur Hebung der untern Volksclasse nebst Bemerkungen ueber den Central-Verein in Berlin* (Elberfeld, 1845).

Harkort's enthusiasm for the principle of association was stimulated in 1844 when the Prussian government, after the shock of the Silesian riots, founded in Berlin a "Central Society for the Welfare of the Working Class." The government intended the Central Society to be the headquarters of a network of societies which were to be organized by local initiative throughout the kingdom. Harkort hailed this movement as the stirring of new life: We stand on the eve of great progress in social relations. The mighty spirit of association is ready through brotherly love to close the broad gap which separates the lower from the upper classess.[11]

When the government, alarmed by the number of radicals who captured the leadership in founding local welfare societies, killed the whole movement with official neglect, Harkort was bitterly disappointed. He did not, however, conclude, like so many other liberals, that effective social action on the part of the government would never come until the government had been made responsible to a popular electorate. Instead, Harkort continued to insist that social and educational reform should have priority over political reform. In an open letter which he published in April, 1849, he remarked: "The participation of the people in political power is achieved more rapidly than the preparation necessary for such participation; therein lies the misfortune of our time."[12]

GUSTAV MEVISSEN

Like Harkort, Gustav Mevissen was a captain of industry with a life-long interest in public affairs.[13] He was

---

[11] Harkort, *Die Vereine*, p. 5.

[12] Berger, *Der alte Harkort*, p. 418.

[13] On Mevissen, see Joseph Hansen, *Gustav von Mevissen, Ein rheinisches Lebensbild* (Berlin, 1906); Wilifried von Eisenhart Rothe, *Die volkswirtschaftliche Anschauungen Gustav von Mevissens* (Giessen, 1930); Johanna Koester, *Der rheinische Fruehliberalismus und die soziale Frage* (Berlin, 1938), pp. 34–39; Jacques Droz, *Le libéralisme rhénan* (Paris, 1940), pp. 247–76. A good contemporary impression of Mevissen

born at Duelken in the Prussian Rhineland, where his father had built up a small but prosperous spinning mill; his formal schooling ended in 1830 when, at the age of fifteen, he went to assist his father in managing his business. Young Mevissen had been a promising scholar, and his rather light duties in the mill left him much leisure to cultivate his mind. Cut off from intellectual companionship, unable to discuss his reading or his ideas with anyone, he began to keep a journal which turned into an invaluable account of the self-education of a young liberal. Mevissen read systematically through the classical literature of Germany, England, and France. To learn more about contemporary French letters he subscribed to *Le Voleur*, which after 1831 became the *Revue des deux mondes*, a periodical which called his attention to the works of Victor Hugo and George Sand, and to French writing on social questions. Articles on French affairs written by Heinrich Heine and published in the *Augsburger Allgemeine Zeitung* aroused his interest in the ideas of Saint-Simon, ideas which he came to know without the gloss of fantasy added by the votaries of the Saint-Simonian cult. Mevissen was convinced by Saint-Simon that the upper classes should take the lead in organizing a society where everyone could enjoy the benefits of modern industry rather than allow industrialization to reduce the masses to the level of wage slaves. This conviction was strengthened by Mevissen's later reading and experience, particularly by his reading in German philosophy and his firsthand observation of industrial development in Germany and Britain.

From his reading of literature, Mevissen went on to dip into the study of history and then to immerse himself

---

can be found in Rudolf Haym, *Reden und Redner des ersten preussischen Vereinigten Landtag* (Berlin, 1847), pp. 225–59. For Mevissen's activities in the 1840's, see an unpublished doctoral thesis by David I. Gaines, "Young Gustav Mevissen and His Times," (Department of History, Columbia University, 1952).

in philosophy. In his journal he recorded the profound effect of Kantian ideas on his thinking. Kant's insistence on respect for individual rights and on the necessity for self-discipline were echoed and paraphrased in its pages. But Hegel exercised a still greater influence on him, for in Hegel the young autodydact found, after years of reading on a variety of subjects in a number of disciplines, a powerful synthesis which provided him with both a philosophy of history and a program for the future. Hegel taught him to regard history as a revelation of the spirit, or mind, as it ordered and improved the material world and to believe that spiritual forces — truth, love, freedom — in the course of history would win out over ignorance, hatred, and tyranny. Hegel's paragraphs on social problems in his *Rechtsphilosophie* may have influenced Mevissen's views on specific questions of social organization, particularly his opinion that industry should be decentralized. But, above all, Hegel inspired this future industrialist with a purpose in life. To translate the ideal into reality, to ensure the domination of matter by mind, to realize spiritual values in public and private life, was for Mevissen, to work for a program of industrial development which would not brutalize the working class but, rather, would improve their condition. The combined influence of Saint-Simon and Hegel made Mevissen's mind proof against the Marxian argument that industrial development under capitalism would inevitably drive the workers into destitution and issue in violent revolution.[14]

Mevissen's thinking on social questions was also shaped by personal experience. In 1836 he went on a business trip through the Rhineland which took him into many of the larger centers of commerce and brought him for the first time into direct contact with some German business

[14] For the influence of Hegel on Mevissen's intellectual development, see Hansen, *Mevissen,* I, 125–38; Haym, *Reden und Redner,* p. 236; Eisenhart-Rothe, *Die volkswirtschaftliche Anschauungen,* pp. 67–68.

leaders. He returned to Duelken depressed and disgusted by the materialism and the hard self-satisfaction of those he met.[15] In the next few years he also made business trips to England, and what he saw there instructed him further in the dangers of free competition's degenerating into brutal and unbridled selfishness. He concluded that individual ambitions had to be curbed and intelligently directed and that the state had some responsibility for doing this, especially when an economy was rapidly expanding under the pressure of population growth. In 1842, Mevissen witnessed some Chartist demonstrations in England and reported back to *Die Rheinische Zeitung* that these were orderly and that the Continental press was exaggerating the violence of the Chartist movement. Nevertheless, in the same reports he was critical of the English upper classes for perverting industry into a system of oppression and for creating a new class which in time of business depression or of crop failure would be driven by hunger into rebellion. In 1846, while visiting the Midlands, he wrote to his wife:

This Leeds is the filthiest spot in all England. Hardly a ray of sunlight comes through the smoke-blackened windows. All the misery of modern industry is heaped up here. . . . Magnificent factories in which thousands of human beings waste away physically and spiritually. . . . What a bright future there will be when one day the grandchildren of these ragged workers demand compensation for the sufferings of the present. . . . Neither the Corn Laws [*sic*], not a great, bloody revolution can lift the curse of the past from this country.[16]

Although he recoiled from the social effects of free competition which he had seen in England, Mevissen was equally dismayed by the alternatives being put forward at that time by socialists in France. Saturated in idealist

[15] Hansen, *Mevissen*, II, 95–99.
[16] Hansen, *Mevissen*, I, 465, n. 1.

philosophy, he reacted with loathing to the materialism of Proudhon. He was interested in, but not persuaded by, the ideas of Louis Blanc.

Organization of work is the slogan of this new movement which believes in the development of civilization through reform of social conditions. . . . The principle of our present-day organization is the free activity of the individual, subject to the necessity of self-preservation and the impulses of egotism. All reform movements start with this principle and seek, in the most diverse ways, to raise the power of the group above the individual, the universal interest above the individual interest. This is possible in two ways: through the use of force by direct government intervention, or through free choice, that is, by a free act of the individual. The first way is a reversion to a phase of civilization which was left behind long ago, a phase in which the all-devouring power of the state was considered an expression of the universal will; this way would lead society to a mechanistic death.[17]

Mevissen did not want to allow the excesses of economic individualism to go unchecked, nor did he want to sacrifice modern gains in personal freedom by restoring medieval restrictions or by establishing a socialist system.[18] As a Kantian, he wanted a society of self-disciplined men who exercised their freedom within the limits of reason and morality and with due regard for the common good. As a Hegelian, he believed that the state should be a vehicle for the progress of reason and morality — more specifically, that the state should educate its citizens to the point where they were capable of leading a rational life — and that the state should enliven the social conscience of its citizens and should mediate tensions between them. This process of education he understood in a somewhat broader sense than did Harkort; it would be an education conducted not only in public schools but through free political institu-

[17] *Ibid.*, I, 181.
[18] *Ibid.*, II, 87–91.

tions. Along with Harkort and Brueggemann, Mevissen believed that Germany, by learning from the mistakes of other countries and by giving wise direction to its economic development, could avoid the terrible social consequences which modern industry had brought to Great Britain. Indeed, Germany, he thought, had a rare opportunity to promote the victory of mind over material circumstance.

The most pressing social problem in Germany in the 1840's, according to Mevissen, was the growth of a rural proletariat.[19] He agreed with Friedrich List that the solution to that problem lay in industrial development and called on the state to encourage capital investment in new industries by providing tariff protection, by supporting a more liberal credit system, and by opening up the mines to exploitation. But industrialization would merely transfer social problems from the country to the towns unless it was carefully supervised. Mevissen was especially anxious for the state to co-ordinate the building of a transportation system which would allow the decentralization of industrial plants. He thought that one of the major causes of working-class misery in England was the concentration of factories in great manufacturing centers with their appalling slums, and he repeatedly urged that German factories be dispersed about the countryside. Ideally, the industrialist in a free enterprise system would not take advantage of his workers, but the state should ensure the workers against any abuses of free enterprise by fixing minimum wage scales and maximum work schedules. Further, in times of depression, the state should provide work for the unemployed in public works projects.

In 1840 Mevissen moved from Duelken to Cologne where he continued his highly successful business career while finding opportunities to take part in some of the

[19] Haym, *Reden und Redner,* p. 245; Hansen, *Mevissen,* I, 177–78, 405–6; and II, 85.

social movements which were beginning to stir in the Rhineland.[20] In 1842 he joined some prominent citizens of Cologne in sponsoring the publication of a daily paper, *Die Rheinische Zeitung fuer Politik, Handel, und Gewerbe,* which was to become a more outspoken liberal organ than the *Koelnische Zeitung;* and in 1844, when the government called for the organization of local societies to advance the welfare of the working class, Mevissen was eager to answer the call. But both the newspaper and the society foundered on governmental disfavor. The *Rheinische Zeitung,* to which Mevissen himself sent reports from England, quickly became a sounding board for some of the most radical voices in Germany: Karl Heinzen, Arnold Ruge, Karl Gruen, Bruno and Eduard Bauer, and Friedrich Engels were among its contributors. Karl Marx, who became editor of the paper in the autumn of 1842, published some articles in December of that year criticizing the Prussian government for allowing the exploitation of the vineyard workers in the Moselle Valley to go unchecked. The government objected; the management of the newspaper apologized. But Marx renewed his attack on the government early in the new year, and the paper's doom was sealed at a cabinet meeting in Berlin on January 21, 1843. Mevissen was well aware of the shortcomings of the *Rheinische Zeitung;* he considered it too negative in spirit and had had little sympathy for the "Young Hegelians" who wrote for it. He also disagreed with some of the radicals who became active in the organization of the Cologne Society for the Welfare of the Working Class in 1844. But the government's heavy-handed methods of dealing with these movements filled him with contempt. In August, 1845, writing to a friend, he remarked on the stupidity of a government which could shut its eyes to the need for

---

[20] Hansen, *Mevissen,* I, 243–81, 347–58; Koester, *Fruehliberalismus,* pp. 39–41.

social reform and at the same time admonish the poor to seek comfort in the biblical message that equality exists only in the sight of God.[21] These experiences confirmed Mevissen in the belief that social reforms could be achieved only after successful constitutional reforms had made the government responsible to its citizens.

During the latter 1840's, Mevissen entered politics; he was elected to the provincial diet of 1846 and to the United Diet of 1847. During that period of bad harvests and widespread unemployment, he did what he could as a private citizen to relieve social distress. Beginning in 1845 he used his position as director of the Rhenish Railway to send trainloads of coal and food into distressed areas where these cargoes were then sold at cost to the inhabitants. But he neither proposed nor worked for any long-range social reforms. Rather, his speeches in the election campaign of 1846 and in the period of controversy over the king's manner of summoning the United Diet show his preoccupation with political issues.[22] All Prussia was excited by the question of the Diet's constitutional status, a question which was argued before it met in April, 1847, and throughout its sessions. The other issues before the Diet which caused the most controversy were the question of government subsidies for an eastern railway and the question of Jewish emancipation. Although Berlin was disturbed by hunger riots soon after the Diet met and although social distress in Germany was probably more acute in the spring of 1847 than at any other time in the 1840's, the members of the Diet were not distracted from their political quarrels.

Mevissen's letters from Berlin, written while he was a member of the United Diet from April to June, 1847, show

---

[21] Hansen, *Mevissen*, I, 358. For Marx's articles of January, 1843, see Karl Marx and Friedrich Engels, *Werke*, I, 354–83; Franz Mehring, *Karl Marx* (3d ed.; Leipzig, 1920), pp. 35–53; Auguste Cornu, *La jeunesse de Karl Marx, 1817–1845* (Paris, 1934), pp. 201–10.

[22] Hansen, *Mevissen*, I, 451–66.

his continued absorption in constitutional problems.[23] He was, however, seated on a committee whose business it was to study recommendations for relieving social distress and to report on these to plenary sessions of the Diet. The committee reported twice. On April 27, its report dealt with suggestions for closer government control of the sale of foodstuffs during the present period of acute shortages. The committee favored only a ban on the export of potatoes and on the use of potatoes by distilleries. A more significant report was made on May 17, when the committee called for state-financed public works to provide jobs for the unemployed, a proposal which was adopted almost unanimously. In addition to speaking for the committee's recommendations, Mevissen supported Camphausen's position in the debate on income tax legislation. But in general he was disappointed with the Diet's failure to consider social problems on a broader scale, which he blamed on the disunity and lack of foresight among the middle-class delegates. Still, he had believed all along that constitutional reform had to be the liberal's first objective in 1847, and after the dissolution of the Diet he remarked that at least that issue had been joined and honorably fought on both sides. He was optimistic that the liberals would win more tangible gains in future sessions and that they would use these gains to press toward a solution of the social problem.

KARL BIEDERMANN

At a Berlin hotel named the Russische Hof, a meeting place of liberal members of the United Diet, Mevissen met and spoke with Karl Biedermann, a young professor and publicist from Leipzig who had come to Berlin to observe the work of the United Diet and to write its history. Biedermann had in common with Mevissen an interest in moder-

[23] *Ibid.*, II, 35–316. For the reports of the committee on relieving social distress, see Eduard Bleich, *Der erste Vereinigte Landtag in Berlin, 1847* (Berlin, 1847), II, 96–131, 735–47.

ate political and social reforms; he was also an ardent
nationalist who had reached the conclusion early in the
1840's that German unification could be achieved only behind Prussian leadership.[24] Born in Leipzig, the illegitimate
son of a domestic servant, Biedermann had an unconven-
tional upbringing which took him first to Brietenhof, a mill
town in the Erzegebirge, then to Dresden, and, finally, back
to Leipzig to attend the university. After a few years at the
University of Heidelberg in the early 1830's, he returned to
Leipzig to qualify as a professor and began to teach an
unusual combination of courses in philology and political
science. Perhaps even more unusual was the fact that his
first major written work was a weighty, but semipopular,
study of German idealism, which he published in 1842.

In his review of German philosophers since Kant, Biedermann tried not only to sum up the ideas of Kant, Fichte,
Schelling, Hegel, and Herbart but to show the implica-
tions of their ideas for political and social thought and to
warn his German readers that these philosophers had the
wrong approach to practical problems.[25] In spite of the
tremendous progress made since the time of Descartes, he
said, speculative philosophers had yet to break completely
away from the ecclesiastical-scholastic tradition which had
given birth to philosophy. They still acted as though all
thought should be a systematic search for absolutes. But
human life resisted the iron grid of logical systems, and in
everyday affairs there were no absolutes. Germans should
be on guard against thinking that ideal freedom or ideal
justice could ever be realized or that somewhere, off in the
distance, they could find an ideal solution for political and

[24] The title of Biedermann's history is revealing: *Geshichte des ersten
preussischen Reichstags* (Leipzig, 1847). On Biedermann, see Karl Biedermann, *Mein Leben und ein Stueck Zeitgeschichte* (Breslau, 1886);
Neue deutsche Biographie, II, 223–24. No secondary study of him has
appeared.

[25] Karl Biedermann, *Die deutsche Philosophie von Kant bis auf unsere
Zeit* (Leipzig, 1842), I, v–x.

social problems. They should rather learn to live in an imperfect world and to make the best of it; they must learn to live not by logic but by the law of life. Biedermann's formulation of that law was somewhat misty; he called it the "principle of free development" and described it in terms very similar to those used to describe Kant's principle of the free self-realization of the individual.

But Kant's arguments for individual freedom had not been logical, and the arguments of Kant's successors for the omnipotent state had been logical. So much the worse then for logic! Biedermann's "law of free development" could be judged by its effects. It fostered a positive rather than a negative morality, advising self-fulfilment rather than self-denial. It nurtured the principles of constitutional government; and leaving behind both vague cosmopolitan yearnings for a universal culture and gentle Christian admonitions toward universal brotherhood, it promoted peace between nations by recognizing differences of language, laws, and customs, at the same time finding beneath these differences a common humanity. But the law of free development had not, Biedermann admitted, been very helpful in securing for men a better material existence. He noted that great increases in productivity had been accompanied by the phenomena of overpopulation and mass poverty, of intermittent trade crises, and of threats of trade wars between nations and class war within them.

But to ascribe these evils exclusively to the principle of free development and to want either to condemn it absolutely, or to confine it within artificial limits would be to rush headlong in the wrong direction, would be to cut by force, rather than to unloosen, the knotty problems of the present. . . . We can not wish to retreat; we must go forward with confidence that the power of nature has a remedy for every evil which may arise, with confidence in the infallibility of our own self-knowledge whose inalienable law is that impulse toward free, unlimited development.[26]

[26] *Ibid.*, II, 738..

The aspirations with which Biedermann concluded his *Die deutsche Philosophie* could not conceal the fact that he had failed to think through his own position on social problems. During the next few years, while engaging in a flurry of journalistic work, he took pains to correct that failure.[27] In 1842, he had founded a monthly review, *Die deutsche Monatsschrift*, as an organ for the nationalism and the empirical liberalism which he had professed in his book on the philosophers. Two years later, he founded a weekly newspaper, *Der Herold*, and after another two years, a quarterly, *Unsere Gengenwart und Zukunft*, which would enable him to take advantage of the "zwanzig Bogenfreiheit" allowed to publications with a more substantial format than the ordinary newspaper or pamphlet. In the winter of 1846–47, he collected statistics on the income and living costs of Saxon workers and published his findings in *Der Herold.* His reading in socialist literature prepared him to write a series of articles for *Gegenwart und Zukunft* under the title, "Sozialistische Bestrebungen in Deutschland." And in early 1847 he summarized his views on social questions in a series of public lectures given first in Leipzig and then, because of their success, at Dresden. These lectures were published from Biedermann's notes and from some stenographic records as *Vorlesungen ueber Sozialismus und soziale Fragen.* They are interesting as a digest of many of the opinions which thoughtful liberals had formed on social questions as of 1847.

In his first lecture, Biedermann emphasized the necessity of understanding socialist and communist movements. They were not just crackpot schemes, they had proved to be capable of attracting intelligent and devoted men to their causes. These movements had sprung up — and here Biedermann joined Schulz and Mohl against Rau — be-

[27] Biedermann, *Mein Leben*, I, 58–174. See also *Unsere Gegenwart und Zukunft*, I (1846), 194–264; II (1846), 207–67; IV (1846), 268–332.

cause of the growth of a proletariat, a class of people who were poor, not because of personal failings or accidental causes, but because the economic system made them so and kept them so. One of the causes of their poverty, to be sure, was a natural one: population growth had outrun food supplies. But new economic conditions had aggravated the problem by separating capital and labor, that is, by making it impossible for the workers to own either the raw materials or the tools they worked with and thus had deprived them of any control over the production or the marketing of the articles they made. Still another reason for the rise of a proletariat was the separation of skill and labor, which had reduced workers to selling only their time and which had brought a fall in wages. Finally, Biedermann observed that liberal political movements had awakened the proletariat to an awareness of their condition, had shown them how to organize in their own interests, and, unintentionally, had sharpened their resentment against the upper classes. The workers in 1846, he said, were asking: "What good is freedom? . . . Does it give us bread?"[28]

Biedermann's second lecture summed up the objections which socialists raised to non-socialist proposals for solving the social problem. Measures to control population growth by banning early marriage or fostering emigration were considered unjust because they required special sacrifices of the poor. The argument, put forward by such liberals as Prince Smith and Rau, that the poor would benefit from industrial growth was fallacious because greater productivity would almost certainly lead to overproduction and the miseries of periodic unemployment. Legislating minimum wages, as suggested by the social liberals, could not succeed where employers were already paying as much as they could without pricing their products out of the market. Only an international agreement on minimum wages would

[28] Karl Biedermann, *Vorlesungen ueber Sozialismus und Soziale Fragen* (Leipzig, 1847), p. 64.

really help, and there seemed to be little prospect of that. For the socialists, then, the social problem was insoluble without a full-scale reorganization of society. Biedermann pointed out that the socialists had certain goals in common with the liberals. Both wanted to establish a fair balance between work done and rewards received; both wanted a system which would bring material prosperity. But whereas the liberals thought that these goals could best be reached through free competition, the socialists thought that they could only be reached by an organization of effort in which the individual would give to society what he produced and would receive back from society what he needed.[29]

In a historical review of socialist systems, Biedermann referred briefly to community efforts whose motives were religious, to "utopians," like Plato, More, Campanella, and Harrington, to *philosophes*, like Rousseau and Mably, and then proceeded to discuss in greater detail the modern socialists. These, he believed, could be sorted out into a few general categories. Socialism, in the strict sense, was a system which sought to regulate individual relationships for the sake of fair play; communism, on the other hand, sought to fuse individual interests in a common interest. He further distinguished two kinds of communism: the *Gleichheitskommunismus* of Étienne Cabet and Wilhelm Weitling, which would use external force to establish equal rights, equal work, and equal rewards; and the *Freiheitskommunismus* of Théodore Dezamy, a kind of anarchism which would rely on an inner regulator to stimulate people to work hard for society and yet also limit their own rewards. Underlying all these systems was the belief that free competition and private property rights must either be abolished or drastically curtailed.[30]

Biedermann cautioned his audience against facile judg-

[29] *Ibid.*, pp. 71–112.
[30] *Ibid.*, pp. 119–89.

ments for or against socialist movements. The socialist proposals should neither be laughed off as impossible nor accepted just because the evils they attacked were real. In his opinion, any fair-minded observer would have to agree with the socialists that private property rights had indeed been abused and that free enterprise had often been debased into a selfish scramble for riches. He was convinced that some reforms were necessary; in fact, they were already underway but were being enacted without the socialist label. The introduction of a graduated income tax, state control of railways, more extensive systems of state aid to the poor, had begun to limit the rights of private property. The principle of association embodied in self-help organizations and relief societies had begun to encroach on the principle of individualism. Anyone who favored such measures, Biedermann maintained, was, to some extent, a socialist, and he advised his listeners not to be afraid of labels but to judge such measures solely on their merits.[31] He left little doubt that in his opinion the merits of such measures were many.

The key to the problems posed by socialism and the social question, said Biedermann, was the question: "How far should the principle of individualism be neutralized?" [32] Should all individual rights be submerged in a community of property, of education, of family life? To ask these questions was to raise the more fundamental question: "Is man by nature a purely social being, who should own nothing, earn nothing, do and enjoy nothing, not even live, apart from social regulations?" [33] Biedermann told his audience that after long deliberation he had concluded that men are neither purely social nor purely individual beings. He found his answer in a concept of personality which distinguished between those moments in life when a man

[31] *Ibid.*, pp. 247–60.
[32] *Ibid.*, p. 261.
[33] *Ibid.*, p. 262.

acted by and for himself and those moments when he acted as one of a group. He believed, for example, that everyone should be independent in setting his goals in life and in choosing the means to achieve them. Once these choices were made, the individual should be ready to recognize that they implied responsibility to the groups with whom he would study and work. The individual should be aware that he could not realize his goals without help from others. But independence, or self-reliance, remained for Biedermann the "vital principle, the essential key-note of human nature," and he predicted that any society which denied it utterly would suffer for it.

In his concluding lecture, Biedermann refused to speculate on the future of socialism; he hoped that social problems would be discussed freely and dispassionately and that reforms would be undertaken. But he advised his listeners not to look for easy solutions or final answers to these problems. Above all, he expressed the hope that political reform would come about before the pressures for social reform grew stronger. The middle classes needed to win political power and to educate themselves in its exercise. Should a working-class revolution break out before then, such chaos would result that no one could tell how soon it would be before peace could be restored to society.[34]

SOCIAL LIBERALISM FIFTY YEARS LATER

Biedermann's later career and the subsequent development of his thought on social questions are worth tracing as a postscript to this account of social liberalism in the irenic days before 1848. Like most liberals, Biedermann was caught up in the political gales of 1848, and political issues monopolized his attention. A member of the *Vorparlament* and of the National Assembly, vice-president of the delegation which waited on Frederick William IV to offer him the crown, Biedermann saw the ruin of his hopes for German

[34] *Ibid.*, pp. 277–78.

unity under Prussian leadership. Yet he returned to Saxony and fought a rear-guard action against the anti-Prussian policies of Count Friedrich Ferdinand von Beust in that state. Dismissed from his professorship in 1853 for political activity, but reinstated in 1865, Biedermann continued to pour out articles, books, and pamphlets which show his preoccupation with politics. After his program for German unity had been achieved, he wrote a history of Germany between 1840 and 1870 in which he devoted only a few pages to social problems after 1848 and then only to praise Schulze-Delitzsch's co-operatives and to express some surprise and anxiety at the development of the Social Democratic Party of August Bebel and Wilhelm Liebknecht.[35]

Not until 1899, more than fifty years after his first series of lectures on socialism and the social problem, did Biedermann return to those subjects, and the change in his attitude toward them is a measure of changes in the times rather than in the man. In this second set of lectures, he reaffirmed his liberal conviction that both historical experience and reflection on human nature taught that society should be so organized as to allow maximum freedom to the individual; but he conceded that in modern society some collectivist laws and institutions were inevitable. He paid tribute to the scholarly work of the *Verein fuer Sozialpolitik*, a society of distinguished academicians which at one time included Gustav Schmoller, Wilhelm Roscher, and Adolf Wagner. These "Socialists of the Chair," as they were called in derision, were engaged in an effort which Biedermann found laudable, an effort to find a middle road between collectivisim and individualism. He also acknowledged the usefulness of such "state socialist" legislation as Bismarck's insurance and compensation laws of the early 1880's. Biedermann was unimpressed by Adolf Stoecker's Christian socialism and Friedrich Naumann's national socialism, but he was dismayed by the Social Democrats who

[35] Biedermann, *Mein Leben*, II, *passim.*; *Dreissig Jahre deutsche Geschichte, 1840–1870* (2d ed.; Breslau, 1883), II, 176–80, 489–98.

were, in his opinion, the real villains of recent German history.[36]

How had the Social Democrats succeeded in winning such power as they had by 1899? They had, said Biedermann, three advantages over their opponents. The Social Democrats were able to contrast the defects and inequities of the present system with the perfection of their hypothetical dream world. Second, they had the initial advantage which always lies with the aggressor; they were always ready to attack, to criticize, to denounce, and could give the impression that they were the only party which had the workers' welfare at heart. Actually that impression was far from the truth, but it had taken hold of the half-educated. Finally, the Socialists had a dictatorial leadership and a highly disciplined party organization. With these tactical advantages, the Social Democrats had succeeded in dividing Germany against itself, in stirring up class hatred, or, at the very least, in poisoning society with suspicion. What could the liberals do to meet this challenge? Biedermann urged them not to fight "a battle of ideologies." Marxist ideas had been discredited long ago by historical events, and even Liebknecht had thrown out the doctrine of increasing misery and the labor theory of value. The strength of the Social Democrats lay not in their ideology but in their organization. Liberals must be as efficient in their organization and as energetic in their campaigns as the Socialists. They must break down the artificial barriers which the Socialists had built around the workers and prove that, in fact, the Socialists had retarded the progress of social reform. Meanwhile, liberals should go ahead with a program of moderate reforms, undeterred by fears that the Social Democrats would overtrump them. Their battle would not be easily won, but their exertions would be worthwhile, for the prize of victory was social peace.[37]

[36] Karl Biedermann, *Vorlesungen ueber Sozialismus und Sozialpolitk* (Breslau, 1900), pp. 141–75.

[37] *Ibid.*, pp. 192–205.

The bitterness in Biedermann's comments on the Social Democrats is understandable. From the beginning of his literary career, he had been warning Germans not to look for easy or ideal solutions to complex problems. How disappointing, in his old age, to see large numbers of his countrymen lured into a sociopolitical movement which made utopian promises on the basis of "scientific" calculations! But the success of the Social Democrats could not be explained exclusively by reference to their tactical advantages and to the gullibility of the people. By 1847, the liberals had the beginnings of a common-sense program of social reform; by their failure to develop the program in the following decades, they abandoned the field of social reform to the socialists. They lost the confidence of the working classes and lost it, in large part, by default.

Conclusion

Marx and Engels in *The Communist Manifesto* dismissed most of the writing on social problems in the 1840's as the work of "economists, philanthropists, humanitarians, improvers of the condition of the working class, do-gooders, members of societies for the prevention of cruelty to animals, temperance cranks, hole-and-corner reformers of every imaginable kind."[1] But this kind of derision tells us more about Marx and Engels than it does about the ideas and proposals they scorned. The German liberals whose ideas on social problems have been the subject of this study produced no new system of metaphysics, no grandiose interpretation of all human experience. They did not pretend to be scientific. In an age of ideologies, their empirical approach to social problems may have appeared weak and unconvincing. But the ability of men like Karl Heinrich Rau, Robert von Mohl, Friedrich Harkort, Gustav Mevissen, and Karl Biedermann to observe the facts of social change and their willingness to modify theories in the face of those facts were in reality sources of strength. For in the long run even ideologues have to come to terms with facts, and the actual evolution of social policies and reform legislation, in Germany and elsewhere in western Europe, has borne out the common-sense recommendations which these men made in the early nineteenth century. In addition to being practical, their freedom from ideological principles

[1] Karl Marx and Friedrich Engels, *Werke, Schriften, Briefe* (Frankfurt am Main, 1927–35), VI, 522.

gave their views on the future of German society a flexibility altogether lacking in doctrinaire socialism. From the point of view of historical determinism, Marx and Engels studied English conditions in order to predict what must inevitably happen in an industrialized Germany. In contrast, the social liberals observed what was happening in England in order to prevent its recurrence in Germany, and thanks largely to the efforts of Gustav Mevissen, the Ruhr district did become the most highly industrialized area on the continent without duplicating the slum conditions of "Black England."

With a realistic view of the problems of population growth and industrialization and with a genuine desire to keep peace between the classes, the social liberals proposed many reforms in common with those socialist leaders who were genuinely interested in curing social ills rather than in proclaiming a revolutionary ideology. As liberals they could hardly support the community schemes of Wilhelm Weitling. Nor could they agree with those associations of artisans and workers who in 1848 denounced occupational freedom. But they could agree to many of the proposals made by Stephen Born and Karl Georg Winkelblech, who as spokesmen for those groups called for minimum wage scales, maximum hours limits, a graduated income tax, free schools and libraries, and welfare benefits for the sick and disabled.[2] Even the more extreme socialists, when anxious to win over the workers to their cause, announced objectives which were identical with those of the social liberals. During the summer and fall of 1847, Marx and Engels in England, and Moses Hess in Belgium, were busy formulating resolutions for the Communist League, a radi-

---

[2] On Weitling, see Carl Wittke, *Utopian Socialist* (Baton Rouge, La., 1950), esp. pp. 56–59. On Born and Winkelblech, see W. E. Biermann, *Karl Georg Winkelblech (Karl Marlo)* (Leipzig, 1909), II, 1–151; Wilhelm Friedensburg, *Stephen Born und die Organisationsbestrebungen der Berlinerarbeiterschaft bis zum Berliner Arbeiter-Kongress* (Leipzig, 1923), pp. 72–74.

cal association made up largely of German exiles. They included in their program such reform measures as the decentralization of industry, an income tax, relief for the disabled, and state-supported schools.[3] To be sure, the members of the League were supposed to regard these reforms as transitional measures, as first steps toward a wholesale reorganization of society, but the very fact that Marx and Engels publicly endorsed them was a tribute to the broad and immediate appeal which such proposals had at that time.

Advocates of social liberalism could also agree with conservatives on specific reform proposals no matter how sharply they disagreed on principles. Some conservatives, of course, faced resolutely backward; Franz Baader, for instance, made a very shrewd analysis in 1835 of social disorders and then went on to recommend that the rifts in society be closed by making clergymen the legislative representatives of working-class associations; Karl Ludwig Haller, as late as 1850, called on Europeans to repudiate industrialism and return to the patrimonial, corporate regime of the Middle Ages. But the less tradition-bound conservatives realized that Europe had entered a new age and was encountering new problems that required new solutions. It is ironic that Mohl's article on the disadvantages of industrialization and the means of overcoming them, published in Rau's *Archiv der politischen Oekonomie* in 1835, became one of the foundations of modern Catholic social thought. In April, 1837, Franz Josef von Buss, a leading conservative in Baden, speaking in the Diet on behalf of factory acts, delivered an address which was little more than a condensation — and in some passages, a paraphrase — of Mohl's article. And, as one historian has noted: "From Buss's speech there is an unbroken chain of thought to the

[3] Marx and Engels, *Werke*, VI, 545; Moses Hess, "Die Folgen der Revolution des Proletariats," *Sozialistische Aufsaetze*, ed., Theodor Zlocisti (Berlin, 1921), p. 220; G. D. H. Cole, *A History of Socialist Thought* (London, 1935–60), I, 219–62.

social sermons of Ketteler in 1848, and from him to the reso-
lution of Count von Galen in the Reichstag in 1877 and
the whole socio-political program of the Center Party."[4]

Probably the foremost theorist among Protestant conservatives in Germany during the 1840's was Friedrich
Julius Stahl. Although it may be true, as W. O. Shanahan
has remarked, that "Stahl dealt exclusively with principles,
not with policies . . . ," he did indicate in one or two
passages of his monumental *Philosophie des Rechts* what
general measures he favored for ensuring that industrialization would cease to be a cause of social oppression, and
these passages are, for all practical purposes, succinct re-
statements of Harkort's opinions.[5] Stahl recommended the
following measures: an expanded system of relief for the
very poor, government supervision of industrial practices
to prevent exploitation of the workers, and the organization of self-help societies. Another leading Protestant,
Viktor Aimé Huber, came back to Prussia from a trip to
England in 1844 and began to campaign so vigorously for
such reforms as the decentralization of industrial plants and
workers' housing developments that Johann Hinrich
Wichern, a prominent organizer of Protestant charities,
feared that Huber had been corrupted by the spirit of
materialism.

By 1847, then, a number of German liberals had thought
out a rationale of social reform and had advanced a pro-

[4]Karl Bachem, *Vorgeschichte, Geschichte, und Politik der deutschen
Zentrumspartei* (Cologne, 1927–32), I, 270. See also W. E. Hogan, *The
Development of Bishop William Emmanuel Ketteler's Interpretation of
the Social Problem* (Washington, 1946), p. 7; Karl Spreng, *Studien zur
Entstehung sozialpolitischen Ideen in Deutschland auf Grund der Schriften
Franz von Baaders und Franz Josef von Buss* (Giessen, 1932), pp. 84–94.

[5] W. O. Shanahan, *German Protestants Face the Social Question: The
Conservative Phase, 1815–1871* (Notre Dame, 1954), p. 254; Friedrich
Julius Stahl, *Die Philosophie des Rechts* (2d ed.; Heidelberg, 1845–47),
Vol. II, Part II, 57–58, 82–83; Victor Aimé Huber, "Ueber innere Coloni-
sation," *Janus*, I (1846), 193–222, 225–55. For the difference between
Huber and Wichern, see Martin Poerksen, *Johann Hinrich Wichern und
die soziale Frage* (Rendsburg, 1932), 95–96.

gram of specific measures which might have won some support from both socialists and conservatives. Why, then, did
the German liberal movement as a whole fail to champion
any such program? Why did it fail to become a mediator
between left and right? One significant reason for this
failure lies in the divisions and distractions which charac-
terized liberal views on the social problems before 1848.

Economic and social conditions in the 1830's and 1840's
presented a confused picture: here stagnation, there progress; now prosperity, then depression. Understandably, the
liberals read the signs of the times differently. The social
liberals themselves differed on whether priority should be
assigned to constitutional or to social reforms. But the crucial split was between the social liberals and the defenders
of economic individualism, between those who saw the
distress of the 1840's as a portent of social revolution and
recommended some degree of collective action and those
who explained away that distress as a temporary maladjustment which a free economy would work out best if left
alone. Easily overlooked in a study of this kind is the fact
that many liberals before 1848 were quite indifferent to social questions. The liberal group in Koenigsberg led by
Johann Jacoby, for example, was too engrossed in clamoring
for a constitution to worry about anything else. One of the
leading intellectuals in western Germany, the historian
Friedrich Christoph Dahlmann, never alluded to the social
problem in his writings or speeches. In 1845, he published
a history of the French Revolution which simply ignored
the operation of social forces and treated the whole upheaval as an exercise in the drafting of constitutions.[6]

Events during the Revolution of 1848 and the period of
reaction which followed it only broadened divisions among

[6] F. C. Dahlmann, *Geschichte der franzoesischen Revolution bis auf die
Stiftung der Republik* (Leipzig, 1845). On Jacoby, see Ferdinand Falk-
son, *Die Liberale Bewegung in Koenigsberg, 1840–1848* (Breslau, 1888),
pp. 118–35; on Jacoby's subsequent shift of interest, see Leonard Krieger,
The German Idea of Freedom (Boston, 1957), pp. 391–92.

the liberals on social questions. While class interests were not as clearly defined in the German revolution as they were in the French revolution of 1848, the fact remains that some incidents in 1848 and 1849 threw a fright into German middle-class liberals by demonstrating the possibility that mob violence could be directed not only against princely governments but against property rights as well. Moreover, the agitation by radical liberals for popular sovereignty conjured up the possibility that the common man, once in power, would use that power to redistribute property by peaceful, legislative methods. These startling prospects "stimulated the bourgeoisie to an intensified consciousness of its own property interests and to resistance against further progress of the revolution."[7] Certainly, after 1848 a large number of German liberals were more suspicious than ever of any proposal for social welfare schemes or government controls which seemed to curtail the rights of private property. Finally, the period of reaction in the 1850's coincided with a spurt of prosperity which dispelled many of the anxieties of the 1840's and appeared to confirm the views of those who had argued that the economy would right itself without government interference. Admittedly, that prosperity suffered setbacks in 1857 and, later, in 1868, but these brought no return to the widespread distress of the late 1840's.

In this postrevolutionary period of business expansion, John Prince Smith came into his own. He took the truth that workers and employers have some interests in common and inverted it into the fallacy that they have no interests which are distinct. Thus, he argued, there was no working-class problem as such; there was only the problem of making society as a whole more productive. And, while the economy was booming and the standard of living rising, that problem seemed well on its way to solution. Mean-

---

[7] Krieger, *German Idea of Freedom*, p. 336. See also Jacques Droz, *Les révolutions allemandes de 1848* (Paris, 1957), pp. 624–31.

while the old principle of economic individualism was restated in terms of "natural selection," taken over from
Darwinian biology. After Prince Smith died in 1875, the
cause was taken up with peculiar persistence by Eugen
Richter, who because of his political power succeeded in
identifying the Progressive Party with a last-ditch defense
of free enterprise.[8]

Meanwhile what of the social liberals in the postrevolutionary era? Harkort continued to promote welfare associations in his corner of Westphalia but did nothing on
behalf of a national reform program. Mohl devoted himself
to writing on constitutional law and to representing Baden
in negotiations for unification. Mevissen and Biedermann
campaigned for better technical training for the working
class but did not do much more for them until the great
political questions had been resolved, questions which they
had consistently held should take priority over social problems. In 1868, Biedermann sponsored an employers' lia-
bility act in the Reichstag, and in the 1880's Mevissen
helped to prepare Bismarck's social insurance legislation,
although he had very little confidence in its usefulness.
The contributions of the social liberals to social reforms
were not negligible, but they were certainly minor.[9]

[8] See, for example, Eugen Richter, *Politisches ABC-Buch, Ein Lexikon parlamentarischer Zeit- und Streitfragen* (Berlin, 1896). On Prince Smith's later publications and on the influence of Darwinian theory on social thought in Germany, see Heinrich Herkner, *Die Arbeiterfrage* (8th ed.; Berlin, 1922), II, 129–45. Both Prince Smith and Richter are discussed in Krieger, *German Idea of Freedom*, pp. 396–97; 407–13. Krieger errs, however, in stating that Prince Smith proclaimed Ricardo's iron law of wages. See above, pp. 87–88, for an explanation of Prince Smith's doctrine of "enrichissez-vous."

[9] Mohl has only a few, scattered references to social problems in his *Geschichte und Literatur der Staatswissenschaften* (Erlangen, 1855–58) and his *Encyclopaedie der Staatswissenschaften* (Tuebingen, 1859); his most scholarly work of this period, *Staatsrecht, Voelkerrecht, und Politik* (Tuebingen, 1860–69), has none. On Biedermann, see *Vorlesungen ueber Socialismus und Sozialpolitik* (Breslau, 1900), p. 7; on Mevissen, see Eisenhart Rothe, *Die volkswirtschaftliche Anschauungen Gustav von Mevissens* (Giessen, 1930), pp. 72–73.

Nor did the social liberals find any immediate successors to take up the search which they had abandoned, the search for a middle way between the extremes of free enterprise and state control. Hermann Schulze-Delitzsch (1808–83), with his self-help associations, was closer in spirit to Hansemann than to Harkort; certainly he had none of Harkort's concern for industrial workers as opposed to artisans. The limits of Schulze-Delitzsch's interest in the working class became clear early in the 1860's when he approved a decision of the *Nationalverein* to reject an appeal for the admission of more working-class members. In 1868, the German People's Party, a liberal organization with considerable strength in Saxony, Wuerttemberg, and Baden, officially adopted some of the proposals for reform put forward twenty years earlier by the social liberals. But this effort to keep working-class support for a liberal political organization ended in failure. During the next two years, 1869 and 1870, August Bebel and Wilhelm Liebknecht broke with the People's Party and founded the Social Democratic Workers' Party as their vehicle for political action by the working class.[10]

Not until 1873 with the founding of the *Verein fuer Sozialpolitik* was there any sustained effort to chart a course of social reform which would avoid the extremes of collectivism and individualism along lines laid down before 1848. The founders of the new *Verein* included some active politicians as well as a number of distinguished academicians who were known as "Socialists of the Chair," or *Kathedersozialisten*. From the beginning, however, the *Verein*, even in its internal dissension, resembled a learned society rather than a movement for social reform. Comparable in many respects to the Fabian Society in Britain, it made great contributions to the study of social problems and to increasing public awareness of these problems; but it could not compete for attention with the Social Democrats, who in

[10] Krieger, *German Idea of Freedom*, pp. 418; 450–57; Herkner, *Die Arbeiterfrage*, II, 353–54.

addition to publishing research studies for intellectuals shouted their slogans at public meetings, spread their gospel through newspapers and pamphlets, and fought for their cause in the political arena.[11]

Social liberalism in Germany began in the 1830's and 1840's as a series of practical responses to problems which had arisen, or were expected to arise, from earlier liberal reforms, from the rapid growth of population, and from the development of new industries. Revived in the 1870's, it sponsored some impressive research projects into social problems. Meanwhile the liberal advocates of laissez faire had succeeded in establishing their views as the "classical" liberal position. The fact that by the mid-twentieth century all of the industrial nations of the West had adopted the kind of mixed economy which the social liberals recommended bears witness to their good judgment. That they failed in the mid-nineteenth century to press for action on their recommendations was a misfortune both for the liberal movement and for Germany.

[11] Herkner, *Die Arbeiterfrage*, II, 164–89. On the *Verein*, see Else Conrad, *Der Verein fuer Sozialpolitik* (Zuerich, 1906).

Bibliographical Essay

I. ECONOMIC AND SOCIAL HISTORY

The best general introduction to German economic and social history is Friedrich Luetge, *Deutsche Sozial- und Wirtschaftsgeschichte* (2d ed.; Berlin: Springer, 1960), which has some terse but comprehensive discussions of the effects of liberal reforms and the reaction against them. By contrast, Heinrich Bechtel, *Wirtschaftsgeschichte Deutschlands* (3 vols.; Munich: G. D. W. Callwey, 1951–56), is more literary and less substantial. Dealing specifically with the nineteenth century, Werner Sombart, *Die deutsche Volkswirtschaft im neunzehnten Jahrhundert und im Anfang des zwanzigsten Jahrhunderts* (7th ed.; Berlin: G. Bondi, 1927), is a series of brilliant impressions inspired by socialist sympathies, which may be supplemented by the stodgier, A. Sartorius von Waltershausen, *Deutsche Wirtschaftsgeschichte, 1815–1914* (2d ed.; Jena: G. Fischer, 1923). The latter, although concentrating too narrowly on developments in Prussia in the early nineteenth century, is a useful introduction to the great serial publications of monographic studies of economic history sponsored by Johannes Conrad, Gustav Schmoller, and the Verein fuer Sozialpolitik late in the nineteenth and early in the twentieth centuries. A still more useful guide to this material is Johannes Conrad and Ludwig Elster (eds.), *Handwoerterbuch der Staatswissenschaften* (3d ed., 8 vols.; Jena: G. Fischer, 1909–11).

Social history as a record of the popular culture, the life of the family, and the community activities of the time may be found in *Biedermeier: Deutschland von 1815–1847* (Berlin: Bruno Cassirer, 1923), by Max von Boehn. Ernst Heilborn, *Zwischen zwei Revolutionen* (Berlin: Wegweiser-Verlag,

1927), is a less graphic essay in cultural history. Georg Hermann [Borchardt], *Das Biedermeier im Spiegel seiner Zeit* (Berlin: Deutsches Verlagshaus Bong & Co., 1913) is a collection of excerpts from memoirs, journals, and other ephemeral writing which may help the reader unlock those stores of social history. Finally, no student of any aspect of German history in the early nineteenth century can afford to ignore Heinrich Treitschke, *Deutsche Geschichte im neunzehnten Jahrhundert* (5 vols.; Leipzig: S. Hirzel, 1879–84), or Franz Schnabel, *Deutsche Geschichte im neunzehnten Jahrhundert* (4 vols.; Freiburg im Breisgau: Herder, 1929–36). Although Treitschke concentrates on political developments and Schnabel on intellectual history, both have occasional passages and many scattered details which shed light on economic problems and social conditions. Schnabel, perhaps because of his association with the Technische Hochschule in Karlsruhe, is particularly good on the development of technology and technical education.

The titles of literary sources and travel books that I found helpful for their description of social conditions are mentioned above in chapter ii, where I have also tried to evaluate their contents; therefore, I need not re-enter those titles or judgments here. Of them all, the most valuable were: Thomas Charles Banfield, *Industry of the Rhine; Series I: Agriculture* (London: C. Knight, 1846), and *Series II: Manufacture* (London: C. Cox, 1848); William Howitt, *The Rural and Domestic Life of Germany* (Philadelphia: Carey & Hart, 1843); and John Strang, *Germany in MDCCCXXXI* (2 vols.; London: J. Macrone, 1836). Collections of statistical data are indispensable to economic and social historians but must be used with caution. There was very little effort to co-ordinate the work of statistical offices in the different states in Germany, with the result that there was great heterogeneity and discontinuity in standards and periods of measurement as late as the mid-nineteenth century. *Geschichte, Theorie, und Technik der Statistik* (2d ed.; Stuttgart: J. G. Cotta, 1903), written by one of the pioneers in the Prussian Statistical Bureau, August Meitzen, discusses some of the crude and misleading methods used there in the early and middle decades of the century and should serve as a general warning. The particular shortcomings of Wilhelm Dieterici, *Der Volkswohlstand im preussische Staate* (Berlin: E. S. Mittler, 1846), are discussed at some length above in chapter ii. The best collection on agriculture is Alexander von Lengerke, *Landwirtschaftliche Statistik der deutschen Bundesstaaten* (2 vols.; Braunschweig: G. Westermann, 1840–41). Two compilations of later date which have useful information on the 1830's and 1840's are: Friedrich Wilhelm von Reden, *Deutschland und das uebrige Europa* (Wiesbaden: Kreidel & Niedner, 1854), and Georg von Viebahn, *Statistik des zollvereinten und noerdlichen Deutschlands* (3 vols.; Berlin: G. Reimer, 1858–68). A combination of descriptive and statistical data, as well as a fascinating example of an early attempt at a sociological case study, will be found in the account of the life of a miner in the Harz Mountains in the 1840's which is included in the third volume of Pierre LePlay, *Les ouvriers européens* (2d ed., 6 vols.; Tours: A. Mame et fils, 1877–79).

A definitive study of population growth in central Europe cannot be written until there is considerably more research into the demography of the various states. Erich Keyser, *Bevoelkerungsgeschichte Deutschlands* (Leipzig: S. Hirzel, 1938), despite traces of racism, is a useful survey. Helmut Haufe, *Die Bevoelkerung Europas, Stadt und Land im neunzehnten und zwanzigsten Jahrhundert* (Berlin: Junker & Duennhaupt, 1936) is a collection of statistics without interpretation or analysis. Particularly helpful for the 1830's and 1840's is Paul Mombert, *Studien zur Bevoelkerungsbewegung in Deutschland* (Karlsruhe: G. Braunsche Hofbuchdruckerei, 1907). August Loesch, *Bevoelkerungswellen und Wechsellagen* (Jena: G. Fischer, 1936), is a classical study of the economic effects of population bulges. Valuable information about emigration in the early nineteenth century is to be found in Wilhelm Moenckmeier, *Die deutsche ueberseeische Auswanderung* (Jena: G. Fischer, 1912). Emigration policies of the different states are discussed in several articles included in Eugen von Philippovich (ed.), *Auswanderung und Auswanderungspolitik in Deutschland* ("Schriften des Vereins fuer Sozialpolitik," Vol. LXII [Leipzig: Duncker & Humblot, 1892]).

The liberal reforms and their consequences have been studied by a number of American historians in books which may serve the interests of those who do not read German. Guy Stanton Ford, *Stein and the Era of Reform in Prussia* (Princeton, N. J.:

Princeton University Press, 1922), provides excellent background material on the emancipation edict of 1807. Walter M.
Simon, *The Failure of the Prussian Reform Movement, 1807–
1819* (Ithaca, N.Y.: Cornell University Press, 1955), although
primarily concerned with political reform, deals briefly with the
emancipation edicts of 1811 and 1816. Carl William Hasek, *The
Introduction of Adam Smith's Doctrines into Germany* (New
York: Columbia University Press, 1925) has brief chapters on
agrarian and trade reforms. Hugo C. M. Wendel, *The Evolution
of Industrial Freedom in Prussia, 1845–1849* (New York: New
York University Press, 1921) is largely a summary of legislation.
Two books which interpret the reforms as instruments for op-
pressing the poor are: Theodore S. Hamerow, *Restoration,
Revolution, Reaction: Economics and Politics in Germany,
1815–1871* (Princeton, N.J.: Princeton University Press, 1958),
and the third volume of Juergen Kuczynski, *A Short History of
Labour Conditions under Capitalism* (4 vols.; London: F. Mul-
ler, 1942–45).

The social consequences of the agrarian reforms have been
discussed extensively by German historians. Theodor von der
Goltz, *Die laendliche Arbeiterklasse und der preussische Staat*
(Jena: G. Fischer, 1893), and Georg Friedrich Knapp, *Die
Bauernbefreiung und der Ursprung der Landarbeiter in
den aelteren Teilen Preussens* (2d ed., 2 vols.; Munich:
Duncker & Humblot, 1927), discuss arguments that the reforms
created a rural proletariat. Erich Jordan, *Die Entstehung der
konservativen Partei und die preussischen Agrarverhaeltnisse*
(Munich: Duncker & Humblot, 1914), presents those arguments
with an impassioned attack on the landed classes. Those who
want a statistical survey of the long-range effects of the reforms
on class structure in rural Prussia will find it in August Meitzen,
*Der Boden und die landwirtschaftlichen Verhaeltnisse des
preussischen Staates* (4 vols.; Berlin: Wiegandt & Hempel,
1868–71). Otto Stolz, "Die Bauernbefreiung in Sueddeutschland im Zusammenhang der Geschichte," *Vierteljahrsschrift
fuer Sozial- und Wirtschaftsgeschichte*, XXX (1940), pp. 1–68,
is a good review of reforms south of the Main. Sebastien Hausmann, *Die Grundentlastung in Bayern* (Strasbourg: K. J.
Truebner, 1892) is a legalistic analysis of successive laws governing the peasants' redemption payments in Bavaria. Otto

Reinhard, *Die Grundentlastung in Wuerttemberg* (Tuebingen: H. Laupp, 1910), gives some attention to political and social influences on similar legislation in Wuerttemberg. A balanced summary of the whole subject of agrarian reform and class structure can be found in Werner Conze, "Die Wirkungen der liberalen Agrarreformen auf die Volksordnung in Mitteleuropa im neunzehnten Jahrhundert," *Vierteljahrschrift fuer Sozial- und Wirtschaftsgeschichte,* XXXVIII (1947), pp. 1–47.

Histories of the reform legislation which introduced *Gewerbefreiheit* into the several states have in general been lawyers' explications of the decrees without much explanation of the ideas and pressures which influenced their drafting. Kurt von Rohrscheidt, *Von Zunftzwang zur Gewerbefreiheit* (Berlin: C. Heymann, 1898), and August Popp, *Die Entstehung der Gewerbefreiheit in Bayern* (Leipzig: R. Noske, 1928), are two such studies. Some attention to public opinion and pressures as they affected legislation in Saxony is given in *Die Entwicklung der saechsischen Gewerbefassung* (Krefeld: W. Greven, 1908), by Paul Horster. On the consequences of *Gewerbefreiheit,* Gustav Schmoller, *Zur Geschichte der deutschen Kleingewerbe im neunzehnten Jahrhundert* (Halle: Buchhandlung des Waisenhauses, 1870), is still fundamental. Schmoller was generally hostile to radical arguments for free enterprise, but in this account he also criticized those extremists who blamed all of the artisans' problems on the loss of guild privileges.

The founding of the Zollverein was the most dramatic development in German economic history in the second quarter of the nineteenth century and has tended, therefore, to divert attention from other developments which favored economic growth. The propaganda campaigns for and against the formation of a customs union have been analyzed in Arnold H. Price, *The Evolution of the Zollverein* (Ann Arbor, Mich.: University of Michigan Press, 1949). Wilfried von Eisenhart Rothe and A. Ritthaler, *Vorgeschichte und Begruendung des deutschen Zollvereins, 1815–1834* (3 vols.; Berlin: R. Hobbing, 1934), is a collection of documents incidental to negotiations between the member states. The best comprehensive study of the founding and subsequent history of the Zollverein is William Otto Henderson, *The Zollverein* (Cambridge: Cambridge University Press, 1939 [2d ed.; London: Frank Cass & Co., 1959]). The role of the Zollverein in promoting industrialization has been exaggerated somewhat in Pierre Benaerts, *Les origines de la grande industrie allemande* (Paris: F. H. Turot, 1933), which is, nevertheless, a work of magisterial scholarship, indispensable to any student of economic growth in central Europe. The treatment of the origins of German industry in William Otto Henderson, *The Industrial Revolution on the Continent* (London: Frank Cass & Co., 1961), is brief but well balanced, drawing as it does on earlier studies by Henderson: *Britain and Industrial Europe, 1750–1870* (Liverpool: Liverpool University Press, 1954), and *The State and the Industrial Revolution in Prussia, 1740–1870* (Liverpool: Liverpool University Press, 1958), in which the author examines the great contributions to German industrial development that were made by British capitalists and mechanics and by Prussian civil servants.

The growing consciousness of social problems in the early nineteenth century and the realization that social distress was spreading beyond the help of traditional caritative or philanthropic agencies have been treated in histories of socialism and socialist thought too numerous to list. Heinrich Herkner, *Die Arbeiterfrage* (8th ed., 2 vols.; Berlin: W. de Gruyter, 1922), discusses many different approaches to the problem, including that of John Prince Smith, but is useful chiefly for those of the latter half of the century. Werner Conze, "Vom 'Poebel' zum 'Proletariat,' sozialgeschichtliche Voraussetzungen fuer den Sozialismus in Deutschland," *Vierteljahrschrift fuer Sozial- und Wirtschaftsgeschichte*, XLI (1954), pp. 333–64, is an excellent analysis of the problem before 1848. William O. Shanahan, *German Protestants Face the Social Question: The Conservative Phase, 1815–1871* (Notre Dame, Ind.: University of Notre Dame Press, 1954), is primarily concerned with changing attitudes among Evangelical churchmen, but also makes some interesting observations on the new dimensions of social problems that the churchmen had to face.

II. German Liberalism

The history of liberal thought and the evolution of liberal movements in early nineteenth-century Germany are best approached through the general histories of Treitschke and Schnabel (cited above in Part I), despite Treitschke's pro-Prussian disdain for southern constitutionalism and Schnabel's corporatist misgivings about the spirit of liberal individualism. Oscar Stillich, *Die politischen Parteien in Deutschland: der Liberalismus* (Leipzig: W. Klinkhardt, 1911), and Oskar Klein-Hattingen, *Geschichte des deutschen Liberalismus* (2 vols.; Berlin: Buchverlag der 'Hilfe," 1911–12), are thin and disappointing on this early period. Federico Federici, *Der deutsche Liberalismus* Zuerich: Artemis, 1946), is an anthology of statements on liberal ideals made by celebrated Germans from Immanuel Kant to Thomas Mann. There are selections from Prince Smith and Biedermann, the latter rather ill-chosen. *History of Political Thought in Germany from 1789 to 1815* (London: G. Allen & Unwin, 1936), by Reinhold Aris, has some useful background material on the origins of both liberal and conservative thought. Painstakingly conceptualized, *The German Idea of Freedom* (Boston: Beacon, 1957), by Leonard Krieger relates the liberals' theories to their political failures.

The German liberals who are the subject of this monograph expressed their views in books, articles, and pamphlets which are discussed in the text and cited in the footnotes of chapters iii, iv, and v above. A brief, systematic review of the ideas of Brueggemann, Camphausen, Hansemann, and Mevissen is available in Johanna Koester, *Der rheinische Fruehliberalismus und die soziale Frage* (Berlin: E. Ebering, 1938). Jacques Droz, in *Le libéralisme rhénan, 1815–1848* (Paris: F. Sorlot, 1940), discusses Camphausen, Hansemann, and Mevissen with less emphasis than Koester on their views on social problems. Two reliable biographies of Friedrich List are M. Bouvier-Ajam, *Frédéric List* (Paris: Librairie du Recueil Sirey, 1938), and Carl Brinkmann, *Friedrich List* (Berlin, 1949). Neither of them, however, is a substitute for Friedrich Lenz, *Friedrich List* (Munich: R. Oldenbourg, 1936), which relates List to his cultural setting in a distinguished combination of biography and intellectual history. Another such combination is *Gustav von Mevissen, ein rheinisches Lebensbild* (2 vols.; Berlin: G. Reimer, 1906), by Joseph Hansen. Mathieu Schwann, *Ludolf Camphausen* (3 vols.; G. D. Baedeker, Essen: 1915), has some biographical narrative mixed with records of the Cologne Chamber of Commerce. Alexander Bergengruen, *David Hansemann* (Berlin: J. Guttentag, 1901), and Karl Wild, *Karl Theo-*

dor *Welcker, ein Vorkaempfer des aelteren Liberalismus* (Heidleberg: C. Winter, 1913), are rather superficial narratives. Gustav Freytag, *Karl Mathy, Geschichte seines Lebens* (4th ed.; Leipzig: S. Hirzel, 1898), is charmingly written but should be supplemented with E. Angermann, "Karl Mathy als Sozial- und Wirtschaftspolitiker (1842–1848)," *Zeitschrift fuer Geschichte des Oberrheins*, N.F. LXIV (1955), pp. 492–622. Angermann's *Habilitationsschrift*, a major study of Robert von Mohl, as well as his essay on Mohl and Lorenz von Stein, "Zwei Typen des Ausgleichs gesellschaftlichen Interessen durch die Staatsgewalt," in Werner Conze (ed.), *Staat und Gesellschaft im deutschen Vormaerz, 1815–1848*, Vol. I (Stuttgart: Klett, 1962), came to hand too late for use in preparing this monograph. It is to be hoped that someday Karl Biedermann will attract the biographer he deserves.

Index

Index